RAISING DAUGHTERS

A Christian Mom's Guide for the Lifelong Journey

September McCarthy

A Christian Mom's Guide for the Lifelong Journey

RAISING DAUGHTERS

MOODY PUBLISHERS
CHICAGO

All emphasis in Scripture has been added.

Edited by Amanda Cleary Eastep
Cover design: Faceout Studio, Spencer Fuller
Cover silhouette graphic of girl copyright © 2025 by Techzaka/Shutterstock (2463879099).
Cover silhouette graphic of mother copyright © 2025 by Lana Brow/Shutterstock (2417260049).
Cover graphic pattern copyright © 2025 by Just Dzine/Shutterstock (2305926903). All rights reserved.
Author photo: Emilee Carpenter

ISBN: 978-0-8024-3374-9

Originally delivered by fleets of horse-drawn wagons, the affordable paperbacks from D. L. Moody's publishing house resourced the church and served everyday people. Now, after more than 125 years of publishing and ministry, Moody Publishers' mission remains the same—even if our delivery systems have changed a bit. For more information on other books (and resources) created from a biblical perspective, go to www.moodypublishers.com or write to:

Moody Publishers
820 N. LaSalle Boulevard
Chicago, IL 60610

1 3 5 7 9 10 8 6 4 2

Printed in the United States of America

To my seven daughters, my daughters-in-love,
and my granddaughters
You are His beloved.
Seek Jesus above all else and He will direct your steps.
When you look in the mirror, remember how much
you are loved.

This book is for you, and for the generations of women who
will come behind us.

I will always love you, no matter what.
Mom and Nonna

Contents

Introduction 9

Part One—Laying the Groundwork: Building Connection to Shape Her Journey

Chapter One: The Mother-Daughter Dance 15

Chapter Two: A Personal Reflection 27

Chapter Three: Grit, Grace, and Godliness 39

Chapter Four: It's the Little Things 59

Chapter Five: An Invitation to Friendship 71

Chapter Six: Girl Talk 85

Part Two—Her Strong Start: Building Connection That Guides Her Growth

Chapter Seven: Habits to Last a Lifetime 105

Chapter Eight: Friends and Boyfriends 121

Chapter Nine: Good Christian Girls 137

Chapter Ten: Preparing for the Future 151

Chapter Eleven: The Changing Roles of Mothers 169

Chapter Twelve: Nothing Is Wasted 185

A Note from September 195

Notes 197

Introduction

MY DAUGHTERS ARE SOME OF my favorite people on earth. No matter their age, I will always see them as my little girls. There isn't an expiration date on my love, time, attention, support, and prayers. Once a mom, always a mom. I look at my daughters and wonder how this much love is possible. While I grieve their grown-up absences, I rejoice daily in their beautiful lives. Before you judge a book by its cover, I want you to know that it has taken me years to embrace being a mother of daughters. I was stretched (quite literally) until I thought I would break. My entire journey of raising daughters from girls to women cannot be captured within the pages of one book.

This relationship is a delicate balance of give and take. You will give until you don't think you can give one more breath; and then one day, they will give in return. Raising girls doesn't have to break you, but you will learn to bend. You will flex muscles of humility, strength, and courage like no other workout has ever afforded you. Though raising your daughters will be different from my experience, that is the beauty in this relationship. There isn't a one-size-fits-all formula for raising girls. You will be her biggest cheerleader, a shoulder to cry on, or a phone call or text away when no one else understands. This is for life. Your daughters will inspire you and heal you. One day, you will be holding them close, their hair damp with your tears, and the next moment, you will be crying on the phone with them because you have become their listening ear and comforter. You cannot try too hard or hold on too tight. You will do some things wrong and not get it all right, but what matters is that you were there.

The purpose of this book is to help guide mothers and daughters through the complexities of growing up and growing together.

My hope is to help us nurture our mother-daughter relationships by fostering spiritual growth, character development, and lifelong connection. It is when we, as mothers, seek Christ and His example for us as women that we are grounded in faith, love, and mutual respect, and our daughters will see Jesus as their ultimate example.

While we unfold the beauty in this mother-daughter journey, we will also touch on the fact that in the history of relationships, those between mothers and daughters can have a bad rap. Throughout the generations, we've come to expect that conflict between mothers and daughters is inevitable and resigned to the belief that "this is just the way it is." Consider how many of your friends have struggled with this relationship in one way or another. I hope to give new life to this sacred relationship. In this book, I hope to help us change the way we think of mother-daughter relationships. We can reclaim what God created to be beautiful, while raising our daughters to be faithful. It doesn't mean the process is perfect, or the outcome will be a guaranteed "success," but we have been given all we need to grow girls with purpose, while carefully avoiding the tyranny of perfection.

Raising daughters can be one of the hardest, most beautiful reflections of who we are becoming as mothers. It is sobering to consider how our daughters begin to resemble who we are becoming in the process of raising them. The truth is, our daughters will get the best and the worst of us. Each chapter will touch on the formative years, and how our fear can meet faith when we feel like we are failing. The chapters end with three sections for you to consider as your part in raising your daughters and passing this hope onto the next generation:

- **A MOTHER'S REFLECTIONS** will capture the truths and ideas from the chapter, then prompt us with questions to ask ourselves. We will look in the mirror, considering who we are and what our daughters see.
- **WHAT'S A GIRL MOM TO DO?** will provide action steps to take as we consider changing areas of our lives.
- **A MOTHER'S PRAYER** will end each chapter. Written for us to carry into our daily lives, these words will encourage us to raise daughters with grit, grace, and godliness.

If I have learned anything over the last three decades of raising girls to be women, it is that my choices, actions, and words have a direct connection to our relationship. Raising daughters is one of the most beautiful experiences, and an investment in which I have poured my heart and life into. What begins as being a "girl mom," with fun and frills, turns into two women living under the same roof, with distinctive styles, opinions, and schedules. This relationship has its highs and lows, but in the end, we just want the best for our daughters. Don't you agree that we could all use a little help?

Let us become mothers who are raising daughters to walk in confidence and character and to remain rooted in their identities in Christ. This requires a mother who will clothe herself in humility and strength. A mother who guards her tongue and speaks life to those around her, will raise girls who speak words seasoned with grace and wisdom. A mother who believes her worth is found in Christ's love has everything she needs to confidently raise her daughter. You have been given everything you need to be a mother of your daughter. Take a moment to look in the mirror, and rather than considering what you see, ask yourself "who" you see. Let's begin there.

PART ONE

Laying the Groundwork:

Building Connection to Shape Her Journey

1

The Mother-Daughter Dance

WHEN I WAS THREE YEARS old, my mom enrolled me in a dance class. I grew up learning the art of dance in a small basement studio, with a floor-to-ceiling mirror and a worn, chalk-dusted warm-up bar that stretched along one wall. As a little girl and a true introvert, I was always nervous to walk into a room of people. So, when it was time to line up at the warm-up bar, I was self-conscious and nervous to walk through a crowd of other mothers and daughters. My mom gave me every reason to believe I belonged there and that everything would be okay.

When we arrived for each ballet class, she would sit on a long wooden bench in a narrow hall, tightly packed with other moms. She had the best, but most uncomfortable, seat in the house. Knowing she had a full view of the dance floor encouraged me to walk in with confidence and to have fun. I loved my ballet shoes and wore them with pride. When I'd see my mom's face reflected in the huge mirror, my insecurity would fade. She would smile and nod affirmingly, even when my confidence was shaky, and I was unsure of my poise.

I loved dance class because I felt like the only dancer on the floor, seen and loved. As I grew in confidence, I stopped looking for my mom's gaze in the mirror but even so, she was always there. When my fears were gone, I began to focus on my form and poise. Even to this day, I remember the day I looked back in the mirror after a class routine, and my mom wasn't on the bench anymore. For a quick moment, my heart skipped a little beat, but I didn't stop dancing. She wasn't there, but she knew that it was time. You see, my mom stayed on that bench until she knew I wasn't looking for her in the mirror anymore and was confident to dance without the assurance of her presence.

There is a special dance that every mother and daughter will experience. I like to think of mothers and daughters as dance partners. Often, the mother is the lead, and the daughter follows. We spend the first part of our daughters' lives teaching them and leading them, all while learning new and important lessons ourselves—like two people who never took dance lessons and yet spend their whole lives trying to keep in step. Just when we think we have the tempo and the balance and have learned to read one another's moves everything changes. We grow, pivot, and learn together. No one ever teaches you the choreography, but here is how it goes: For every move a mother makes, her daughter is watching. She will choose to copy, repeat, or choose her own way. A mother's reaction will dictate the next move. Every mother sets the tone of her relationship with her daughter.

She can lean in gently to the process of the steps it will take to learn who her daughter is, carefully considering what her daughter sees in the mirror. This dance is unlike any other, requiring sincerity, humility, genuine respect, and unconditional love.

This full-length mirror is an image to always keep before you as you raise your daughters. The mirror always reveals the truth, reflecting our actions, and our motives. Our girls will know and see us for who we are. The moment you first hold that little girl in your arms is the day you begin your beautiful dance. At some point in your relationship, everything you have ever taught them will give them the confidence and the strength to dance on their own. Then we will be the ones to notice they are not looking for us in the mirror anymore.

Your Value Is in Christ

There will be seasons in your dance when you will step on one another's toes, forget your moves, and be out of sync or rhythm. Sustaining your relationship will require you to practice the moves, fix the problems, and focus on the potential. Those three habits will allow you to stay connected, even when you may think they do not need you anymore. After years of trying to stay in step with my girls, I think we have found a good rhythm. I have spent a lot of sleepless nights praying my way through how to fix small conflicts with my girls, asking the Lord to help us get through seemingly small misunderstandings, so we can maintain a strong relationship. We had to fix our attitudes, be honest, and committed to keeping current in our communication. Most importantly, we stay focused on the person we know one another to be. Always thinking the best. My own childhood did not lead to a sustainable relationship with my mom. These experiences seeped into my own identity and how I approached my first years as a mother to my own daughters.

I come from a long line of broken mother-daughter relationships. My mother has walked in and out of my life for many years. I have learned the dance steps of avoidance, fear of abandonment, and pleasing others. It wasn't until I took a long look in the mirror two years ago that I saw where my own brokenness was inhibiting my deep connection with my daughters. For every lie I believed about myself, I would hesitate to reach into the deep recesses of my own girls' hearts because I couldn't believe or see the truth of my own value or identity. I believed the lie that I wasn't a good mom, a great mom, or a loved mom.

Distance or silence threatened my assurance that my relationships with my daughters were okay or secure. I feared what they thought of me or that I was always disappointing them. The chain of lies continued to affect a relationship I had invested everything into with the goal to not carry the brokenness into one more generational line. What was I missing in this pursuit? I was working so hard to be sure I didn't repeat the patterns of broken relationships, but while doing so, I hadn't taken the time to see where those actions were coming from.

The mirror always tells the truth, and the truth will set you free. For me to fully receive the love in these relationships I had given my life for, I had to first believe I was loved, no matter what. I found freedom when I stopped living in the fear that I would not be a perfect mom. Looking in the mirror, I had to stop waiting for my mom's presence and remember who God created me to be. I am His daughter, fully loved, never abandoned, and once I was clothed in this full assurance, I could break and release the broken chains that have held our long line of women captive. I will always grieve my mom's absence because she is my mother. Though I grieve the brokenness, I have been made whole through the process.

There Is No Perfect Mom

The world has created idealistic versions of what being a mom is. Women seem to be given choices of which version of mom they would "like to be." Stereotypes come in all shapes and forms: working mother, stay-at-home mother, helicopter mother, soccer mom, devoted mom, and cool mom. Sure, we find our people, our style, our groove. We can choose to stay home or a career, and yet, we are and always will be "mother"—the woman up at night cradling her baby, wondering if she will ever see a full night of sleep again. A mother bears heartache and carries pride when her children do hard things, overcome obstacles, win an award, or make new friends. A mother feels every fiber of her child's pain and celebrates every milestone because her children are not only part of her, but they are also a major part of her life.

With seven daughters, I have learned that there is no one way to be the best girl mom. Because my daughters are so very different, my relationship with each of them is unique as well. From the moment I held them in my arms, I knew they would each need me uniquely, and I would love them all so differently. When I learned to see myself the way God sees me, I was able to give my girls a gift I am not sure they are even aware of yet. I gave them the gift of acceptance and uninhibited love. I began loving them without expectations. I thought the best of them when they were silent or busy. I rediscovered how I love and need to be loved. I cheered them on, was present when I could be, and didn't function out of guilt when I couldn't be. As exhausting as it sounds to lavish attention on your daughters, it is also just as suffocating to them, and your relationship. Your daughters want you to be happy and whole. This is how you break the chain of broken relationships. It is not just your actions that are important. You need to heal the wounds and lies you've believed about yourself.

Your family may not have a line of broken mother-daughter relationships, but some of us do. Right now, whether you are raising little girls, middles, teens, or young adults, your future is in the mirror. Your young girls have the potential to be your best friends someday. The trajectory for your relationships is being set in your everyday moments. Do not underestimate the impact your own identity and personal healing will have on your future.

Motherhood Will Transform You

Are you ever prepared for the moment you become a mom? Books and experts tell us what to expect, sometimes through negative stories or fear-based advice. Motherhood is also celebrated with well wishes and gifts. Whether planned or unexpected, the journey to becoming a mother never really prepares you for the moment you hold your child and realize that this, in fact, is forever. Nothing will ever be the same, including yourself. Your body has been changing, your time is not your own, your thoughts will always be interrupted, and you are now in charge of a precious, beautiful life.

My older girls and I basically grew up together. Looking back, I recognize how different I was when they were born. They watched me learn how to mother them. I made mistakes and experienced small victories. They watched me learn so many "girl" things—from braiding hair to putting on makeup. I learned and they watched, as I taught myself how to cook from scratch, plan and grow a garden, and fill my shelves with healthy food for my family. I studied midwifery and took courses with two toddlers in tow and a baby strapped to my chest. I learned how to manage a home and create community. I discovered the importance of my health, skin care, and nurturing my femininity. Everything I did and learned turned into a teaching moment for my daughters.

Being a mother of daughters reminds me of the intricate beauty woven into our DNA as women. While I watch my own youth fade away, I behold the beauty of my daughters unfolding before me. I see them learn and lean into their womanhood.

Being a mother has pushed me to get out of bed, and some days, to embrace rest so my daughters know it is okay to choose which they need most. Being a mother to daughters has brought me to my knees, realizing how selfish I can be. Because, yes, I do want some days and some moments to be about me. Don't we all? We want to be present yet need a break. We want to teach them everything they may need to know, but they may make it difficult. They ask for our help, but only when they are ready to receive it. They want to hang out, but only when it's convenient. We must learn how to be both friend and mother. We know their fullest potential, but they cannot see what we see, and so our words must be careful, timely, and sensitive to their seasons.

Motherhood has changed me from the inside out. With every child I had, I became more and more aware of the transformation taking place in me. I found courage where I once felt fear. My love expanded, and my ability to listen, rather than always speak out, caught me off guard.

Raising girls is also a daily look in a full-length mirror. You will hear your own words when your daughters speak and your actions when they react—from the tone of our voice, the attitudes you display, the pace in which you live, and the choices you make. Daughters remind you who you are, as you watch them live out what they've observed you do. There is a raw and revealing vulnerability in raising girls because you cannot hide your insecurities or your doubts.

How do we raise strong, independent, sensitive, and well-rounded daughters without losing sight of who God called us to be as individuals and not only mothers? Choose to press in and prepare them to steward all they have been given. Give yourself grace in the learning and enjoy the teaching moments. Don't see everything as a task, but instead as an opportunity to learn together. Let them see you flourish and thrive. Let them see you smile and laugh. Embrace womanhood, and all the changes it brings. Speak with wisdom, let them see you fail with humility and get back up with perseverance.

Let Them See Jesus in You

Sometimes, we will lose sight of who we are while living out our role as a mother. We forget that we are growing, changing, and becoming someone as well. Deep within the confines of our souls—who we believe we are, how we see ourselves—those are the pieces our children see when they see their mothers. They get the best and the worst of us. They watch us change and grow. They witness the sacrifice, the testing of our patience—our words rolling off hasty tongues—and the sanctifying work of growth that is only seen by those closest to us.

As a mother of seven daughters, I haven't been a perfect girl mom. Each of my girls would tell you that I lost my cool, forgot to teach them things, and didn't "do" everything right. I have had seven opportunities to get this dance down, and yet, there were so many days I was clueless, tired, and giving it the best I could. There were moments I would find myself striving to create the perfect mother-daughter relationship, and yet, I felt like I couldn't quite figure out what I was doing wrong. Mother-daughter relationships can be tricky and personal. From the beginning, we are responsible to train, teach, love, laugh, show up, give space, and prepare them to be women, while at the same time, we are evolving and changing ourselves.

But, at the end of the day, realizing my missteps and knowing I can talk to my daughters about hard things became a lifeline for us. Our daughters are looking in a mirror every day and at the end of the day, all I want is for my girls to see Jesus. We cannot hide who we are from our daughters. The biggest gift you can give to your daughters is to not make the story about you but to stay focused on what God created you to be—a daughter of the King.

Raising daughters is a divine gift to show them Jesus. Be the reflection of Him they see clearer than any other. We have been given a rare and amazing gift to raise the next generation, lead families in a legacy of faith, and to be called a woman of God. Let's reclaim our mother-daughter relationships, so we can raise faith-filled daughters who can confidently know they are loved.

A MOTHER'S REFLECTIONS

- What are my hopes and dreams for my relationship with my daughters?
- How does being an image bearer of Christ relate to my role as a mother?

- When I look in the mirror at the end of the day and my personal relationship and investments into my daughter, what do I see?

WHAT'S A GIRL MOM TO DO?

- Discover the beauty in your own womanhood and how God delights in *you*. What is unique about the way He made you?

- Make a list of the fears you have about raising daughters. Are there generational lies or conflicts you need to identify and give to the Lord?

- Write a letter to yourself and address it, "Dear Daughter." Speak truth to yourself as a daughter of Christ, loved and cherished. Encourage yourself to be open to transformation, with reminders to be an image bearer of Christ to your own girls. Pour your heart out when it comes to your fears of raising girls, your hopes and dreams for your future, and save your letter to read when you need a reminder that you are loved.

A MOTHER'S PRAYER

Dear Lord, I am in awe of Your creation. You have given me the name "Mother," and You call me Your beloved daughter. I seek Your presence as I understand my purpose. I am inclined to doubt my womanhood as beautiful and hover in the shadows of doubt in my motherhood. I know Your Word to be true, Your plan to be perfect, and Your purpose for my life to be worthy of praise. Help me shake off the lies, doubts, and fears as I step fully into Your purpose and womanhood as a daughter and mother to the next generation. Help me to receive and believe Your steadfast love and faithfulness and to see who and whose I am every day. In Jesus' name, Amen.

2

A Personal Reflection

DO YOU KNOW THE FAMOUS quote, rephrased, "Mirror, Mirror on the wall, who's the fairest of them all?" from the movie *Snow White and the Seven Dwarfs*? Every day, the evil queen consulted the mirror for reassurance of her beauty and worth. Until one day, her mirror told her the truth, revealing what was hidden beneath the surface. The mirror never lies.

Over the years, I have forced myself to take a full look in the mirror. I'll be honest and say, I haven't always liked what I've seen. Naturally, my mind gravitates to consider just how much my body has physically changed over the years. My body carried and gave life to babies for two decades, and it's no secret that menopause can wreak havoc on any good effort put into your outward appearance. When I look in the mirror, I have trained my eyes to settle longer on the places that bear stretch marks of love. They reflect a sacred beauty like no other; not to be ashamed of.

I often notice the changes I need to make, and the not so fantastic places I've ignored. You know the places I am talking about. Our eyes almost always see the negative about ourselves first. For every ounce of well-meaning intention, we all have a carry-on case of lies we believe about ourselves that we must choose to let go, or we'll carry them into our motherhood. Lies of identity, self-worth, strengths, or weaknesses are like a chain-link fence, not easily broken. We can become so comfortable in our patterns of brokenness that they become a part of our DNA. Our daughters are living in the overflow of our actions and reactions, making our pursuit of Christ even more important.

Let's take our eyes off our daughters for a few moments and consider our own space of mothering. When we are handed our daughters, no one tells us how deeply personal the calling to raise beautiful, strong, confident, and godly women will be. It is as if in those very first moments, we forget about us and begin the lifelong journey. We stop considering our purpose and begin living out a plan of survival and checklists. But what if we did some preparation work for the calling we have been given? By taking a deep look in the mirror of truth—and seeing ourselves as worthy and valuable and passing this baton to our daughters in confidence and hope. Somehow, culture has created its own standard, making motherhood increasingly more difficult to live up to. We have created a job title with its own set of checkboxes and have resigned ourselves to an outcome based on these lists. What if we circle back to the beginning of who we truly are, before we relegate our failures, our shortcomings, or our inabilities and stop making our motherhood about the checklists we have created?

Before I gave birth to my first daughter, I had the most realistic dream: I was sitting in a chair with my own daughter, while my mother and grandmother were telling me how appalling it was for me to breastfeed my baby, that cloth diapers were the only way, and to be prepared for the worst. Of course, this was only a dream, right? In the years to follow, I stumbled my way through raising seven girls with absolutely no guidance, help, or assurance that I was good enough to be a mother. In fact, I was told just the opposite. Whenever I had a doubt about raising my daughters, I was reminded of the long line of mother-daughter brokenness. The bad dream had become my reality, and I now had seven daughters and three sons to raise. Every day, I wondered how I was going to be a "good enough" mom to my girls. When I looked in the mirror of my motherhood, all I could see was the list of expectations I had put on myself, paired with the list of failures and doubts others had handed to me. When we need Jesus more than we need accolades and others' approval, our self-sufficiency, doubt, and the heroic picture we or others have created for us fade.

The telling moments are when things don't go our way and our daughters mirror our very words and actions. This is when we realize it is time to look in the mirror and learn who it is we want to be like. Because, when it's all said and done, being "good enough" is not enough.

I have known amazing girl moms. I always wondered what in the world I was going to "do" with seven daughters. God knew about my own broken mother-daughter relationship, right? Didn't this disqualify me from doing this well? Could I be trusted to raise daughters who loved God, others, and life in general? How would I ever be good enough to be like those amazing girl moms? It was a deep seed of doubt I had from the beginning. I had seen mothers and daughters share special moments, even share their clothing. I heard their laughter when they were shopping together. I watched moms make matching clothes for their girls, take them on special outings, and braid their hair with precision and pride.

I grew up the oldest of three, with two younger brothers. As they played football, wrestled around the house, and shared the same friends, I did not. I didn't have a sister, and my mother and I were different in every way. My days were spent studying, reading, and writing. I kept my hair simple, never braided, didn't wear makeup, and didn't go on shopping trips or excursions with my mom or other girls. The quality time I needed was lost somewhere over the years in my home, and my "girl world" was minimal at best. Fast-forward to marriage and babies, seven daughters and three sons, and I was clueless as to how to mother my girls.

Let's lay it all on the table here. Raising daughters is wonderful and excruciatingly painful at times. There are days when I feel like I have finally "figured this out," and other days when I feel like an alien living someone else's life, raising someone else's daughters. One of the most surprising things I learned while raising daughters is that just when we think our daughters want us to be involved and engaged, when they are asking for our help and inviting us into their emotional and physical worlds, we are suddenly not welcome. We become a little too close for comfort and they decide they need their space.

I don't know why this surprised me; I am the same way. I like my space, but I also love meaningful relationships. Mothers just need a superpower of intuitiveness and a shield of armor so that our toes won't get stepped on. Like I said, wonderful, and yet excruciating at the same time. Which leads me to share a good piece of advice: "Get yourself some good steel-toed shoes." Your daughters may unintentionally hurt you. They are still learning the ways you show deep love for them and may not realize the personal investment you have in their success and stability. Your dance will be a little less painful when you're prepared for those toe-stepping moments.

My second piece of advice? "Don't quit before you begin." This is where your bravery and humility need to shine. Stop and take a long look in the mirror. When we stop to consider how God sees us—complex in design, fully equipped for our callings, in need of Him every moment—we will daily grow in the strength and beauty of biblical womanhood. It takes bravery to look into a mirror of truth, remembering what God says about His creation, women, character, and abiding in Him. It takes work and humility to know that raising daughters will feel so very personal yet will never really be about us.

Every day, choose to see the best, and leave the rest. Our human nature is to throw up our hands and let defeat win. Your daughters need you to believe what God says about *you*. They need you to lean into the strength He has equipped you with. Your daughters need you to do the work of "you," so you can be the best dance partner God created you to be.

The Mirror of Truth: How God Sees Me

When we face the real questions we have had about our identity, we will need to have answers for our girls. Taking a long look at those areas before or while we raise our daughters is the most important work we can do—because daughters will see our reflections for what they are—and it is vital for them to see Jesus and His work in our lives rather than the empty vices and man-made checklists that the world and comparison will bring our way. If we wait until we have "arrived," or feel "good enough" to be a mom, we may as well raise the white flag now. Womanhood is hard enough, and then on top of it, our daughters will be watching our sometimes difficult and lifelong sanctification. They get a front-row seat view to all God is and will be doing in our own lives as women. It is in the flourishing of us as a woman that our daughters will see Jesus' reflection and want more of what they see.

A personal reflection of who Christ made us to be requires us to seek this truth in His Word, drowning out the world's small talk and endless man-made checklists. His Word is sufficient for our personal transformation. Below, you will read a personal statement for reflection, paired with a specific verse.

Because of Jesus Christ and His work of redemption, **I am deeply loved, completely forgiven, fully pleasing, and totally accepted by God. I am empowered and equipped** by the Holy Spirit to do all God has called me to do.

"You were washed, you were sanctified, you were justified in the name of the Lord Jesus Christ and by the Spirit of our God." (1 Corinthians 6:11)

I have been chosen.

"He chose us in him before the creation of the world." (Ephesians 1:4 NIV)

I am forgiven and free.

"Therefore, there is now no condemnation for those who are in Christ Jesus, because through Christ Jesus the law of the Spirit who gives life has set you free from the law of sin and death." (Romans 8:1–2 NIV)

I am cared for and worthy to be loved.

"Even the very hairs of your head are all numbered. So don't be afraid; you are worth more than many sparrows." (Matthew 10:30–31 NIV)

I have great significance as a child of God.

"See what great love the Father has lavished on us, that we should be called children of God! And that is what we are!" (1 John 3:1 NIV)

The Lord has chosen me to be His treasured possession. My worth is not based on what others think of me, but on what God thinks of me—and He thinks I'm priceless.

"Out of all the peoples on the face of the earth, the LORD has chosen you to be his treasured possession." (Deuteronomy 14:2 NIV)

I am never alone. Jesus is always with me.

"God has said, 'Never will I leave you; never will I forsake you.'" (Hebrews 13:5 NIV)

God has wonderful plans for my life.

"We are God's handiwork, created in Christ Jesus to do good works, which God prepared in advance for us to do." (Ephesians 2:10 NIV)

God has given me everything I need to do all He has called me to do.

"His divine power has given us everything we need for a godly life through our knowledge of him who called us by his own glory and goodness." (2 Peter 1:3 NIV)

Jesus understands what I'm going through.

"We do not have a high priest who is unable to empathize with our weaknesses, but we have one who has been tempted in every way, just as we are—yet he did not sin." (Hebrews 4:15 NIV)

God loves me greatly.

"This is love; not that we loved God, but that he loved us and sent his Son as an atoning sacrifice for our sins." (1 John 4:10 NIV)

God will never forget me.

"Can a mother forget the baby at her breast and have no compassion for the child she has borne? Though she may forget, I will not forget you! See, I have engraved you on the palms of my hands." (Isaiah 49:15–16 NIV)

The Beauty of Beholding

My youngest daughter seems to see me in a way I don't usually see myself. As I hunch over my desk in a corner of the room—a worn winter hat pulled over my head and my reading glasses perched on my nose—writing furiously away on this very book, she whispers across the room, "You are so pretty."

My eyes skim the top of my glasses to focus on her lying on the couch watching me. "Who are you talking to?"

"Mom, I am talking to you. You are so pretty."

I take off my glasses, wipe away tears, and say, "Thank you, honey. You have no idea how timely those words are to me."

The saying must be true. "There is beauty in the eye of the beholder."

I take advice from my daughters now. It seems the tides have turned. Don't be surprised when you begin caring about their opinions and asking for help with your appearance or decisions. This is the beauty of raising daughters. I trust my daughters' opinions, and I am grateful when they share them with honor and sensitivity.

I won't pretend that the last two years have *not* been unkind and non-respecting to my body. Menopause is no joke, and as I learn to navigate these changes, my daughters have had a front-row seat to the mental and emotional toll this has taken. Three months ago, I went to bed to find a handwritten note on my pillow—from my youngest daughter. At the top of the note were the words, "Your Glow Up Plan." Cue the tears. It's okay, you can cry too. With muted pastel and earth-tone journaling pens and highlighters, she had carefully constructed a plan for my body, soul, and mind, with notes and a schedule to follow. She detailed how many glasses of water I should be drinking in a day. (Hey, isn't this what I have been telling my girls daily for the last thirty years?) Her plan included my protein intake, step count, sleep needs, phone usage, skin care, my Bible reading, breathing exercises . . . and the list continued.

Who does this? I will tell you who. The youngest of seven daughters, who has seen her mama's body bear the physical effects of birth and beyond and who knows her mom is weary of trying to show up faithfully in all things. My daughter made me plan, and I am following it like a good mom should. She wants to see me thrive and be healthy. She cares for me, and she invested in me with everything she knew.

I have never felt beautiful. I never believed those words to be true for me, and it is still a daily work of believing it even today. This year, I spent a special weekend away with my seven daughters and my two daughters-in-love. This is my special name for the beautiful brides that married my sons and became my new daughters whom I love. We made time for rest, fun, and great conversation. I relished every single moment and captured so many special memories I will never forget. On one of the evenings, we spontaneously left the hotel in our comfort clothes, drove to a magical ice cream parlor with a brick wall courtyard, twinkly lights, and the feel of a warm summer night, where we all ordered our favorite flavors and sat for a few minutes of conversation. I sat on the outer edge of the circle of daughters and was given a gift of beholding. I listened to them laugh together, talk about babies, life, their dreams, and family. Although it was just a moment in time—I was able to see the product of my life and their lives in full bloom and what a beautiful thing this is to behold. I witnessed womanhood coming full circle and saw each daughter as a unique child of God, who has called them as women to showcase His glory and purpose. It was beautiful.

I am beautiful. Womanhood is beautiful. Do we believe this is what God sees in us every day?

"For we are his workmanship, created in Christ Jesus for good works, which God prepared beforehand, that we should walk in them." Ephesians 2:10

A MOTHER'S REFLECTIONS

- How do I think or feel Christ sees me? How does Christ truly see me?

- What do my daughters see when they see me? What do they hear when I speak?

- How can I draw near to Jesus and reflect Him to my daughters?

WHAT'S A GIRL MOM TO DO?

- Pick one holy habit to put on this week. Keep track of the reflection and difference this will make in your daughter's reactions and responses to you.

- List and identify your doubts as a girl mom and the areas you need to understand and believe for yourself before raising the next generation.

- Make a list this week of the beauty your daughter reflects of Christ and tell her what you see daily. This is not flattery but calling out the reflection of Jesus in her.

A MOTHER'S PRAYER

Dear Father, Your beauty and design is perfect. Help me to believe in Your purpose in my womanhood. May I embrace my motherhood, my body, my calling, the changes, and the reflections of Your image in my life to the world and to the next generation. In Jesus' name, Amen.

3

Grit, Grace, and Godliness

I DIDN'T CATCH THE CUES right away, but my first daughter was not going to fit into the "frilly and pink, craft-loving, shopping daughter" mold. My first clues should have been her aversion to playing with toys and her uncanny ability to lead her brothers into creative adventures (a.k.a., trouble.) My first-born daughter loved climbing trees, playing all the sports, riding four-wheelers, and building things in the garage. She also had an amazing ability to sift through emotional drama. I had been given a leader, a dreamer, and a doer as my first-to-raise daughter.

I had no idea what I was doing. We were different in most every way, and I quickly realized I needed to figure this out. Thankfully, I found my way. I discovered God's way for her, and for us, but the journey had its ups and downs. I learned quickly that this was not going to be a fairy tale that would include ballet shoes hung on the wall next to the tutus or the shopping trips with matching clothes and special lunches that would help us bond.

I was caught off guard when the expectations I had were quickly dismantled. As a daddy's girl, she was more comfortable holding a drill in her hands, being in the woods, or finding a new outdoor adventure. She loved being creative and didn't think out loud. She wanted a camera in her hands and not a book. She raced against the boys and didn't stand by to let them win. In school, she ran for class president and received awards for strength, determination, and leadership. She didn't care about princess parties or dancing with me in the kitchen when I cooked. As she grew, she chose strategic fun, picked her friends wisely and not by popularity, and didn't care about makeup, jewelry, or the fanciest wedding dress. As I write these words, I am smiling ear to ear as I consider her beauty today; she's all grown up and the most amazing woman and mother. I am in awe of her daily.

Together, we found a balance in all the most important things. We created a dance that worked for both of us. She became the oldest of seven girls, and she taught me how to be a better girl mom to her sisters. When I consider the gaping holes that the Lord filled in for me while raising seven different girls, I cannot help but give Him the praise and the glory. He took my expectations of what raising daughters "should" be like and turned them around in the form of the very personal question, "What should *I* look like?" The mirror will always tell the truth.

Don't get me wrong; I didn't do it all right. I learned that raising a girl with different interests and abilities than my own was going to be okay. Every year was a learning curve, and as time slipped by, I held on to three important things:

1. She would know God created her and had a unique purpose for her.
2. She could be a strong leader, but she would still need to be able to do other things that were not her own interests or natural inclinations.
3. She and I may never be the same, but that didn't mean we couldn't have a strong relationship.

My first daughter is a grown woman now. She has a beautiful family and is now raising her three daughters. We have a long line of girls in our family, and believe me, there is no one-size-fits-all mold. The world doesn't need a carbon copy of who we think our girls should be. As mothers of daughters, we can enjoy a healthy and happy relationship, while fostering their unique skills and interests. Will it be easy and feel natural? Not at all. We can get so mixed up in our expectations and ideals, that we forget we are raising girls for His glory, not to fulfill our own identity needs and dream-girl checklist. We can raise independent and creative daughters, with grit, grace, and godliness, but it will require us to take ourselves out of the center of the story. As I continue to raise my last three girls and form unique relationships with my four adult daughters, I can narrow down these top three character qualities to be the overarching themes of who our girls could become.

The Three G's

Raising girls in today's culture can be one of the most challenging, complex, and I daresay, confusing responsibilities. We are met with agendas of reverse male and female roles and messages of "girl power." It is important for us to be prepared with the truth and the ability to walk our girls through the different voices and the noise of the world. Because for every conflicting message the world is screaming at them in full volume, there is always a little thread of truth woven into the messages that appeals to our daughters. Women can be strong, yet gentle. We can lead, and model grace. We can be in the world, and not of the world. Raising daughters with grit, grace, and godliness will require modeling and teaching our girls that how we live today will affect our lives tomorrow. It is our job to model, practice, and teach these things to our girls as they grow.

Grit

I spent a lot of time helping my grandma around her house when I was growing up. A finely spoken phrase she often said to me while we did household chores, side by side, was, "Sometimes you just have to grit your teeth and do it." As a young girl, I never really understood what she meant by this. We canned her garden vegetables in the peak of the summer heat. We changed bed sheets, first washing them and hanging them to dry in the full sun, and then folding them corner to corner together; crisp and flat we laid them in piles. We washed windows, pulled weeds, made fresh squeezed lemonade for guests, and took turns cleaning the garage.

As a child, I didn't see the value in this hard work and perseverance, balanced with special moments of reward and enjoyment. I would just grit my teeth and show up with diligence. I learned the lessons that a good work ethic and attitude reap rewards of inner strength and the fruit of our labor. This is grit. The beauty in giving 100 percent when we can and learning the value of perseverance. Grit not only blesses our personal lives but can affect those around us. I wanted my daughters to know the value and blessing of grit.

We may think of strength as doing demanding physical tasks, but raising daughters with grit isn't just about physical ability. Grit can be the mental and emotional strength that gets your daughter through impossible situations and trying times. Let's not confuse grit with bold and brazen social media messages that tell our girls they don't need a man to be strong. Grit is a character quality that can be seen in a woman when she has a goal and needs extra strength to persevere, or the stamina to be hardworking in a world that screams to women, "Me first." Can we raise daughters who can enjoy the fruit of their hard work and still consider others? Will our daughters have confidence that allows them to try new things and know it is okay to make mistakes?

Work Ethic

My husband and I have raised all our children with the same work ethic. The girls didn't have a different set of chores than the boys, and everyone worked equally as hard as each of their siblings. This was drastically different from the childhood home I grew up in. I was the oldest and the only girl in a family with two younger brothers. I found myself quickly relegated to the "girl jobs" and activities, while my brothers were set apart to do their own things.

The home my husband and I created has been a balance of a good work ethic and trying to raise each of our children according to their own gifts, strengths, and weaknesses. We always focused on teaching our kids formative character qualities, like diligence and perseverance, which we knew would give them the backbone to accomplish any job or task they'd ever be faced with. Our girls have mowed our large lawn, with a self-propelled push mower along our steep back hill, washed dishes by hand without the luxury of a dishwasher, and taken on new skills, even when they didn't want to or think they could. We would never give them an impossible job, but we didn't excuse them from hard work because they were girls. Our daughters grew up knowing we would teach them how to do new things and walk alongside them when it was hard and uncomfortable. They discovered that diligence and perseverance could become part of their DNA when they demonstrated a solid work ethic through dedication and confidence. Daughters do not just "suddenly become" hard-working women, persevering through trials in trust and speaking with words seasoned with grace and godliness.

We've raised our ten kids in a one-income home. This was a personal and intentional decision we made as a couple when we first started our family. There was never a "woe is me" mentality, and we adjusted our life decisions around our self-employed status. It worked well for us, but it wasn't the reason we had our children pitch in to help around the house. The work ethic we chose was intended to develop character and maturity in our children and any extra work they participated in was not done out of lack but a part of our goal. But amazingly, our God does use our lack to teach us grit. The humbling offering of what we do have, mixed with what we cannot give, allows a space for us all to work hard and be humble in this process.

Living in the middle of the woods afforded us opportunities to teach the benefits of hard work. Every time a winter storm hit our area, we had to shovel our way out of our long driveway through the trees. Living in the northeast means you either own a reliable snowblower or have ten children with their own shovels. We, of course, fell into the latter category for many years. Dressed in their snow gear, every one of our kids showed up bright and early to shovel before the rest of the world began their day. As their mom, I didn't like waking them up to the cold and the hard work. I wanted to keep them inside where they were comfortable and cozy, and I couldn't wait to get that long-awaited snow blower. Often knee-deep, or sometimes waist-high, the snow provided the perfect opportunity for the boys and the girls to turn their snow shoveling into a contest. My husband would tell me this was "good for them," while I thought that it was a bit much. Learning to step back and truly assess if the work we were asking them to do was important. Knowing it is reasonable, tolerable, and safe is vital. We cannot re-create the value of our children doing the hard work.

One of the most important lessons in raising my girls to do hard things wasn't just giving them the work to do but teaching the valuable virtues of diligence and perseverance and also the rewards in the fruit of our labor. Sure, my kids loved the delicious hot cocoa and marshmallows and the fully cleared driveway at the end of a labor-intensive morning. They could see the result; the goal had become reality. We all benefited from their physical endurance and efforts. But, in the end, it was their attitudes that defined their actions, and their heart posture that kept them safe from resenting the value of work. As a mom, raising daughters and sons, I never once kept the girls inside because this was the boys' job. We all just pitched in because grit is about knowing the value of work and the worth it brings to others' lives.

Inner Strength

A quality of inner strength can be beautiful in a girl, a woman. It is quiet and hidden until it is needed to help us make decisions and stand firm in resolve and unshaken when necessary. It may seem counterintuitive, but the grit of inner strength shows up as steadfastness and peace. It is part of a woman's beauty, causing the world to wonder what is different. A girl's identity is in question today more than ever before. Her confidence in who she is or will become is being attacked from every corner. Peer pressure speaks in a voice of conformity, and social media sets the tone for the conversations in our daughters' feeds, telling them they must be loud and speak up to be seen, heard, or valued. Remind your daughters that hard work pays off and the rewards are inner strength and confidence. Show them the value of showing up, not giving up, and not being afraid to try or learn new things. Give them the tools to feel the accomplishment of working hard, and the character to enjoy the challenges.

I have daughters who thrive and enjoy working outdoors and with their hands, while others give 100 percent to their academics. They work hard to perfect their craft, or they help pave the pathway to their futures. It is important to teach our daughters to chase after their natural leanings and whatever they put their hands to. But equally valuable is the idea of working hard in areas that they don't enjoy, think they will ever need, or may be difficult for them. This is the point in the journey of raising daughters that requires us, as their moms, to learn to do the hard work ourselves. We will be challenged to either choose a path of least resistance or model grit ourselves. There will be tasks or skills our daughters do not enjoy or things that don't come naturally. We will need to encourage them to do hard or uncomfortable things, even when they don't see the reason for them. A day will come when they realize the value in those experiences, the day when they are putting to use something they had to work hard for but seemed useless at the time. We are always preparing our daughters for the future.

Doing the Hard Things

One of my daughters has a beautiful voice. She is a true extrovert and shines when it is time to plan an event or connect people together. But, when it is time for her to use her gifts and abilities out loud and not just in the background, she becomes paralyzed with fear. Her fear had become a comfortable place for her to land. When asked if she would sing up in front at church or school or asked to lead a group of her peers in a devotional, fear and a lack of confidence threatened to disable her abilities. *Couldn't my older sister do this instead?* she asked, the one who isn't inhibited by being in front of people and makes it all look so easy.

It would have been easier for me to go along with this request. Then, I wouldn't have had to be the "mean mom," encouraging her to practice and prepare. Everything in me always wants to default to pleasing my daughters. I want to avoid the conflicts that come when I know that doing new things will be hard for my children. But is that really helping her use the talents she has been given? Would it have been easier for me to tell her she didn't "have to" do hard things and to not worry about it? There have been hundreds of moments like these in my journey of raising daughters. With everything in me, I wanted to shield them from the critics, allow them to avoid hard things, and give them a pass when life was uncomfortable.

Preparing our hearts and minds ahead of time to go the long road with our daughters when they will need to try new things requires a resilience and balance of love and support. We can tenderly walk with our girls when we know they are facing situations way out of their comfort zones. When my girls have areas of their life that have been untapped or unused, I begin with a conversation about their strengths and interests. Don't be surprised to find their interests lining up with those talents and abilities God has given them but that also come easy for them. We are the same, putting off exercise if we enjoy reading more, or not attending social functions if we are introverted. Our human nature is to avoid challenging situations. Our minds tell us we can't. You will probably hear those same words come from your daughter when you suggest they lean into something new or hard. This is where we take the next steps of instilling courage.

Sometimes, the tasks before them are not about what is easy or hard, but what they must do. They may have to work through a conflict with a friend, stand up to peer pressure, or step out of their comfort zone. Either way, it is our job as Mom to encourage them with words of reassurance when the going gets tough. We can provide tools to equip them, Scripture to stand on, and a shoulder to lean on. Doing hard things makes us all stronger. We become women equipped with grace to raise daughters with grit. Grit shines above the rest, because it is never about us, but about who we are becoming more like every day.

Grace

A mix of dread and regret filled the pit of my stomach. Dread carried me to my knees in prayer, desperate for control over my tongue and the inward lack of self-control that would lash out in frustration toward my daughter. Did she deserve the overflow of my inward battle with being overwhelmed? My knee-bent talk with Jesus overwhelmed me with conviction. I knew my daughter hadn't deserved my reaction, and it was too late to take it back. As I slowly walked my apology back to my daughter's room, I found her curled up against her bed, tears streaming down her cheeks. Bent low, I gently moved strands of hair away from her face and looked into her eyes. "I am so sorry I yelled at you. I shouldn't have reacted that way. Will you forgive me?" I will never forget the silence that lingered between us for a few moments. What felt like eternity, a desperate hope for her to not hold on to this pain, was the moment God was giving her grace to extend to me. "I forgive you."

Six powerful words—"I am sorry" and "I forgive you"—are the first deposits of grace we can give one another. Mothers will not always get it right; in fact, rarely. Grace gives us both a powerful source of healing and a starting point of connection to help us engage with others. Grace provides freedom from the past and expectation for the future. Grace allows us to let go of the striving and extend to others the same grace we have been given—not only between a mother and a daughter, but for us all. Grace rounds off our rough edges, allowing us to conform to the image of God. It is only with His sacrifice and Spirit that we can show kindness when we have been wronged. Our daughters will follow our lead in living a grace-fueled life, living by the power of the Holy Spirit in our words, thoughts, and actions. How we treat those who have wronged us, and what we do with our hands and hours in a day are all on display to our girls. Our speech can be seasoned with grace and not gossip, showing our daughters the overflow of God's work in our imperfect lives as we abide in God's grace and truth.

Grace is something we are given freely. As we choose to see others and our circumstances through the lens of Jesus, we are continually changed and actively living out the grace given to us. We often categorize grace as undeserving forgiveness, which most of us struggle to show consistently. Grace surprises us, as it is unmerited, yet can abound when we choose to extend it to others daily in our actions and our words.

Kindness

Kindness is attractive, and raising kind girls can be a challenge in a culture of spoil and gain. Kindness is an action by which our daughters can extend grace, evidenced by how they see and treat others. Raising kind and thoughtful girls will take intentionality and gentle guidance. It can begin with our words and how we speak to our family and to others outside of our homes. Kindness transfers not only in our words, but our actions. There are different seasons in a girl's life when kindness may come easier than other times. When our daughters are little, their relationship with us is sweet and adoring. They trust us and want to spend time with us, and we enjoy the sweet moments of watching them love unconditionally. Our daughters will grow in their independence and develop relationships outside of their core mother-daughter relationships with us. Every one of our daughters will be faced with complex choices with her friends, her words, and her character. Kindness will become an exercise daily.

When someone gives us grace, we are humbled, and often shocked. We know we are undeserving, and often convicted, knowing that we ourselves might not have been so generous toward others in our own behavior. Grace isn't natural but is supernatural. God gives us what we need and when we need it.

There are different seasons in a girl's life when kindness may come easier than other times. When our daughters are little, their relationship with us is sweet and adoring. Their words and actions are unassuming and often reflect kindness. But, as our daughters get older, entering the middle and early teen years, their social circles grow, and they begin to face complex choices with their friendships, their words, and their character. Kindness will become an exercise, daily.

These are the seasons we can engage in conversation and help guide how they think and react to others. When a girl grows up in a home that models gentleness, kindness, and grace, they can filter their personal friendships and interactions through this lens. Mirroring grace in your home from the time they are little girls will help mold their hearts to be grace-filled girls.

"A soft answer turns away wrath, but a harsh word stirs up anger." (Proverbs 15:1)

This verse reminds us that our words are attached to our emotions and reactions. When your daughters watch you hit pause on your words, catch yourself in a circle of gossip, or handle conflict correctly, they are learning to adorn themselves in grace.

Choosing grace-filled responses will not come naturally to us. When I step back and consider how my daughters speak and treat one another, it is a good baseline for me to consider how I am modeling grace to them. Grace comes from our own belief system of what we ourselves deserve. I ask myself if I am viewing them through the lens of Christ's love for us.

Training our girls to see others the way Christ sees them is the first step to laying a foundation for raising daughters to become women of grace. Helping them forge an identity rooted in His love gives them the security to love others in the same way.

Let's not confuse grace with a quiet reserve that never speaks up. Grace is this amazing quality that can weave gentleness and boldness into a conflict when needed. When my oldest daughter was in high school, she was friends with everyone. The "in-between friend," we called her. She could be friends with the quiet, the unsure, the confident, and the overly confident. She could hold the middle ground of conversations and conflict. I remember one school day when my daughter came home visibly upset. It took a while to pull the story out of her about what had unfolded in the hallway at school. She began by reminding me that one of her classmates had invited her to a birthday party. Supposedly, this was an "invite only" party, and she had made the list. Unfortunately, she didn't know this was an exclusive party until school that day.

While in front of her locker, packing up for the day, she was talking to some of her friends who hadn't been invited. The birthday girl and a few invited friends passed my daughter's locker and said out loud for everyone to hear, "Can't wait for the party. See you there!" My daughter asked the friend hosting the party if she had a minute to talk. By now, both sides of the whole girl gang were stopped in front of my daughter's locker. There were those invited and those who weren't, now all aware of the big special invite-only party. This is where the practice of grit and grace enters the conversation, as my daughter told her birthday friends that she wouldn't be able to attend unless the few girls selectively left out were also included. An immediate quiet and awkward silence filled the hall. Grace had won the hearts of those who were struggling to be kind. Her confidence that kindness would win opened the door to new friendships and set an example of the love the Father has for all His children.

Grace covers wrong with a redeeming measure of hope for any situation. Exhibiting grace to help resolve conflict in this moment forged new friendships and brought a solution to a situation that had been saturated with unkindness. Give your daughters a language of grace: body language, kind and wise words, and the eyes to see others the way Jesus sees us.

Godliness

I fear that perhaps we sometimes fall into the habit of using the word "godly" loosely. When we teach our girls about godliness, we may oversimplify what the Bible tells us to consider. We tell them:

"Be godly."

"Do the right thing."

"Show godliness."

And our daughters are wondering what this means specifically in different life scenarios and how they should act. Maybe this is where we all get lost. We think that godliness is behavior and actions, when rather, being godly comes from within. What we know about God and who He is are the examples set before us. The more time we spend with Him and in His Word, the more we begin to reflect His presence in our life. Godliness is where we find a gentle confidence in who we are in Christ. Godliness honors others as children of Christ. Gentleness and honor are two defining qualities of godliness that our daughters can grow in, but only as they spend more time with God and His Word.

Gentleness

Sometimes gentleness is equated with a quiet reserve or being weak and submissive. Today's culture tells women they need to speak up, be bold, and be their "own woman." There is nothing wrong with speaking up, but let's not mistake the godly qualities of being a good listener and having self-control as less than. The virtue of gentleness stands out among loud voices, demanding attention to have their voices heard. Gentleness leaves room at the table for other women to sit and ask questions, share their heart, and be present.

Can we show our daughters the strength in a gentle spirit that listens and considers others with honor and respect? Gentleness isn't about being quiet, and strength isn't shown by how loud we speak up or how many people take notice. Gentleness stands firm in truth, allowing others to speak, while not speaking over or against. A woman's words are more than the things she says. Her strength is a portrait of confidence in her identity and what she believes. A woman of strength practices patience in her responses, leads with kindness, and shows generosity to others.

There have been moments in my journey of raising daughters when I wished I had been the louder, more demanding voice, knowing my daughters watched other moms speak up for what they thought their daughters deserved. Their intentions were most likely well-meaning, but their approach was loud and void of tact and discernment. I slowly learned over the years that gentleness and kindness win. They are victors over regret and shame. I watched other girls hide in the shadows of their mom's loud demands or embarrassing scenes. I wanted my girls to know that strength comes from walking in the fruit of the Spirit by modeling forbearance, self-control, and long-suffering.

My girls began to see the cause and effect of quick and hasty words. They watched women with the loudest voices become the least respected voice in the room. Seeing strength redefined is important in today's culture. We want our daughters to have the tools and character to speak up when needed and to become better listeners. This world will try and knock them down. Their standards will be questioned. Their identity will be threatened, and their voices silenced. Let's give our daughters the tools to be confident women, showing the world that a gentle spirit equals strength and honor.

- Speak with kindness. Let your daughter hear a gentle tone when you are frustrated or upset.
- Be a safe place. Show her what it means to be empathetic and approachable.
- Care for others. Demonstrate this by considering others' needs and circumstances.
- Apologize and extend grace to others.
- Handle disappointments or change with grace and not complaints.
- Learn how to handle conflict with meekness and humility. A soft answer goes a long way.

"To speak evil of no one, to avoid quarreling, to be gentle, and to show perfect courtesy toward all people." (Titus 3:2)

"Let your reasonableness be known to everyone. The Lord is at hand." (Philippians 4:5)

Honor

When we boil it all down, we want to raise daughters who will bring honor to the Lord with their lives. Their words and actions are not only about them and those closest to them. They are a living example of Christ, for the world to see. Bringing honor to God with our everyday actions is just as important as the goals and aspirations we have. Women can get so caught up in "feeling strongly" about something that we forget our lives are pointing back to Jesus in all we say and do.

We know that living by example is the first step to raising girls with good and godly character. Honor is the long game. I always remind my daughters that doing the right thing will not always reap immediate results or even be easy or feel good. Choosing to do the right thing, in a different way, can often feel isolating. Being the strong yet gentle voice in the room can challenge even the most confident.

Here are a few ways I did my best to model and teach my girls what true strength and honor looks like every day.

- Put others' needs before your own.
- Show integrity. Honor your commitments and be reliable.
- Carry yourself with dignity and confidence. Show modesty in your appearance.
- Respect others in your speech. Avoid gossip and value others with your words.

Verses to Meditate On

"God is in the midst of her; she shall not be moved; God will help her when morning dawns." (Psalm 46:5)

"But they who wait for the LORD shall renew their strength; they shall mount up with wings like eagles; they shall run and not be weary; they shall walk and not faint." (Isaiah 40:31)

"The Lord is my strength and my song, and he has become my salvation; this is my God, and I will praise him, my father's God, and I will exalt him." (Exodus 15:2)

"Strength and dignity are her clothing, and she laughs at the time to come." (Proverbs 31:25)

"But let your adorning be the hidden person of the heart with the imperishable beauty of a gentle and quiet spirit, which in God's sight is very precious." (1 Peter 3:4)

"A gracious woman gets honor, and violent men get riches." (Proverbs 11:16)

A MOTHER'S REFLECTIONS

- How am I modeling gentleness to my daughters every day?
- Am I giving them tools to become slow to speak and to work with diligence?
- Do I allow my daughter(s) to persevere through challenging situations, or do I try to rescue her from opportunities to develop grit?

WHAT'S A GIRL MOM TO DO?

- Observe the way your daughter speaks to her siblings or peers. If there are areas for growth, first take stock of yourself and how she may be reflecting your own tone or words.

- Take note of how she approaches a task or something difficult. Identify opportunities to help her grow in grit.
- Does my daughter take her commitments seriously? If needed, have a conversation about honor.

A MOTHER'S PRAYER

Lord, Your Word reminds us how to be more like You. Help me to live out the fruit of the Spirit in my life for my daughters to see what it looks like to be a woman of strength and honor. May her heart be drawn to the beauty in living a life that brings You and others honor. In Jesus' name, Amen.

4

It's the Little Things

I WALKED INTO THE LIVING room to see her nose pressed up against the cold window, her gaze fixed on the light and fluffy snowflakes that had been falling for hours. She was already dressed in her ballet leotard and tutu, and her pink ballet bag had been strategically set aside by the front door. Her quiet and thoughtful stance told me she was worried that ballet was going to be canceled. She was right: Ballet was canceled. As magical as the snow was, it brought some tears to my little girl's day. We talked about how sad it is to miss the things we love. We had hot cocoa with marshmallows, and I played beautiful ballet music, as my sweet girl did a ballet show for the family. We were living in a snow globe, like a scene from *The Nutcracker*, with a tiny ballerina moving to the music of life. It's the little things.

Our little girls loved ballet. I could have easily focused on the hours of commitment or the price tag on the pink tights, the backup pair of pink tights, the bobby pins in bulk for the buns, hairspray, and backpacks filled with snacks. No one keeps track of the hours spent driving to lessons and sitting in a cold upstairs studio, watching their child's progress through the year. As I stood alongside other moms with my face pressed against the glass of the double door, I was able to take forever snapshots in my mind of my daughters' tiny, pointed toes and their gaze toward the window to see if I was watching. Every single week they asked me if I saw their twirls and spins. Even though they knew I was watching them, they wanted to hear me say the words, "I saw you dance today, and you did a wonderful job."

Recitals showcased their hard work. For me, it was more than ballet. I saw the little things. From walking out on stage without my coaxing to holding their chin up high, I told them every time I noticed their effort and growth. The girls memorized their dances because they practiced relentlessly at home. One overcame her fears and conquered her spins. The other outgrew her ballet shoes, her toe poking through a tiny hole before she told me. Her new shoes were slippery and didn't quite feel the same, but I told her she would be okay if she kept her focus on the most important thing. She loved ballet and I loved watching her.

At the end of every journey in raising girls, we have captured a showcase of the "little things."

Little girls love little things, and although we think those opportunities wax and wane as our girls begin to grow up, they just become bigger little things. Your daughters won't stay small forever, but the magic of creating a moment in time for you to connect is always right in front of you. You don't need fancy trips or high-pressure experiences to connect with your daughters. The little things are moments of intentionality when we lean in and connect where and when we can. Once our girls grow up, they don't need us as much or in the same way. Finding the little things while *they* are little will take work and intentionality. You will notice the open invitations, but other times, you will have to look for them.

In a home currently with three teen daughters, I am sometimes overwhelmed with the constant chatter and conversations. I don't think a book about daughters would be complete if I didn't mention how much talking comes with raising girls. Sometimes, it is about anything and everything. So, when my home is quiet, I know something is off. I usually give my girls the time to work through matters of the heart and mind before I swoop in and try to help. Some girls will tell you everything, and then there are those who don't see the need, or just plain don't want to. A visit to their bedroom is usually at the top of my "little things to do" list. I'll gently knock to see what they are up to, make my way to their bed, and get comfortable, letting them know I am not planning on leaving anytime soon.

"Hey, when did you rearrange your desk? I like it!"

"Thanks. A week ago."

"Your bed is so much comfier than mine. Can we switch?"

I get a smirk. Progress.

"How's your friend doing? I know you mentioned you haven't heard from her in a while."

Silence. Struck a chord.

"Oh, sorry. We don't have to talk about that If you don't want to."

Silence.

"I'm going to town to get coffee. Want to come? My treat." (Don't act too excited or work too hard at this invitation. They are smart and will turn you down.)

(I wasn't planning on going to town, but I am now. It's the little things.)

Pause. "Sure."

"Okay. I'll meet you in the car in ten minutes."

Take selfies. Sip the coffee. Act casual.

"Yah, I haven't heard from my friend. I don't know what to do."

"Do you want to talk about it? Sometimes that helps."

"Yes."

Coffee and conversation can make everything better.

A wave to our little ballerinas at the window can make everything better.

It's the little things.

How They Love

You may be the girl mom who loves to dress your daughter up, take her out shopping, plan special activities, and spend quality time in the kitchen, baking your great-grandmother's recipes. Your daughter may be the kind of girl interested in the great outdoors, photography, playing pickleball, or doing a puzzle, and not interested in small talk.

This is pretty much my version of raising girls, studying seven different personalities and rotating seven unique ways to show them my love. The merry-go-round of adapting to everyone's interests and personalities can get exhausting, and most days I give up before I try. I think this is where some mother-daughter relationships begin to develop cracks. Find the common ground, and if you can't, simply be present.

My adult daughters host the best craft and creative nights once a month for all the girls in our family. They rotate hosting in their homes, and everyone brings whatever projects they are working on at the time. The volunteer host cooks up simple and yummy snacks for everyone to share, and we all gather around the dining room tables, crafting away. All my girls are creative, artistic, and all around talented in that department. I can barely paint or draw a circle, but I try. I have been experimenting in simple watercolor painting, and I have always loved embroidery. My daughters rotate between painting by numbers, assembling miniatures, crocheting, or knitting, editing photos, embroidering, or pressing flowers. Despite my lack of creative ability, I am always welcome at my daughters' tables. My daughters-in-love are always part of the big circle, and someday soon, my granddaughters.

My girls love hosting, and anything that has to do with hospitality. This was our common ground as they were growing up, and it still is today. Many times, while all the girls are crafting away, I just pause and listen to their stories, their hearts, and we laugh and share for a few hours every month. The little things I have learned about my girls in this language of love we all share have been some of the best moments. I may not be a creative genius, but I am present while they do what they love. Learning to notice and enjoy the little things gives us a big and beautiful trajectory for the future. Life is always in the little moments. Learn the language of common ground. You may not know if it is your thing until you try, but really, the most important part is that you are together.

Learning how to love our daughters well is a lifelong journey. Their interests and needs change as they grow. Just because my daughter may love quality time, and I am in a season where I am already feeling stretched thin, I find creative ways to show and tell her how much I love her. With so many girls, the way I love them each will differ from one daughter to the next. Giving myself grace in this process is one of the biggest lessons I had to learn. "Keeping up" with all their needs isn't possible, even with the checklist I had created to spend time with them. Sometimes, we are our own worst critics. Loving our children uniquely is a challenge and meeting all their needs and being available whenever they want or need you is unfair to everyone.

Your daughter knows you love her; here are clues to how *she* loves.

For the girl who shows up wherever you are or wants to be with you no matter what you are doing, she loves quality time. Even when you are busy, the intentional moments of conversation, eye to eye, asking how her day was, or taking her with you to get groceries will fill her love language tank. My daughters who speak this language of love are low maintenance.

They love being with you, or should I say, someone. My daughters who love quality time would honestly be okay to spend their time with anyone. Rather than seeing this as a slight to myself personally, I've learned to recognize that my daughters enjoy being with me, but they haven't made me their everything. Moms, this is so healthy, and it's not about you. These types of children enjoy being with people. Sure, time with you is important, and now you know how to connect with them uniquely, but this is how they love everyone. So, make the time when it works for the two of you. This may look like unplanned windows you have set aside as your "me time" or the errands you'd plan to run alone. Let your children ride along; let them cook with you in the kitchen. Live in the moments you have, give of your time, and someday your children will make space in their lives and schedules for you.

For the daughter who lives life according to lists and Post-it notes, she will know your love by your actions. When you find yourself helping her change her room around, picking out new paint colors, printing off coloring sheets, and you're elbow to elbow helping her organize and clean out her closet, you are loving her well. Sure, this often feels like you are always in "helper mode," and doing work, rather than something enjoyable and fun. Not everyone loves the same way, and this is a perfect example. When you hear the words, "Thanks, Mom," you know she notices your love for her. She may never understand or fathom the depth of your sacrifice for her, when you are adding more work to your already busy life, but she knows you love her because you gave her your time and help when you could. Keep healthy boundaries with your time while loving your daughters through service. Some day you will need help managing a project or remodeling your home, and this will be the daughter who shows up as your right-hand girl. Love is like a circle, always giving back.

Time and attention are your most precious commodities, but your greatest assets. Someday, your daughters will know the great sacrifice you have made, not just because you are their mom, but because of how much you love them. Loving our daughters is an example of how Christ loves us. Putting in the work and modeling sacrifice and selfless love encourages our daughters to love others well. They are watching, even when it seems they may not be paying attention.

I have kept this verse in Hebrews in the forefront of my mind as I have learned to love my daughters uniquely. This truth has helped me remember to encourage my girls in love:

"And let us consider how to stir up one another to love and good works" (Hebrews 10:24).

Learning to Listen

My senses are on high alert twenty-four hours a day. I truly believe this is because I have raised ten children, seven of them daughters. This job should come with an "emotion detector," just to make the guesswork easier, and to give me notice of an impending storm or front of emotion on the horizon. My girls share most everything with me, and when they don't, I don't take it personally. There are big things that are important for us to stay engaged with and little things that aren't going to affect the trajectory of my daughters' lives.

Listening is the "biggest little thing" you can give to your girls. From the time they are toddlers, until they are grown, learn to listen. Our default is to talk, correct, help, or push for an answer when we engage. I have learned that in an effort to fix things or control an outcome, my words seem to be the first and foremost effort to a solution. Rather, I would encourage you to remember my hard learned lesson that things have a way of working themselves out, and my voice doesn't have to be the loudest in the room. Listening is an open door to a larger conversation later. Little moments of listening will keep you engaged in your daughter's life. Begin by asking questions and allowing her to answer in a safe and non-reactive environment. Listen to what she is saying on repeat. Her heart will give itself away. You might have trouble not giving advice every time she opens up about the things going on in her life.

There will be days when her attitudes and actions indicate you are the last person she wants to talk to or be around. Don't let that get to you, and don't try and "teach her a lesson" by not being available when she does return for a listening ear. One day you will be her confidante, and the next day you might as well not exist on her planet. Listening is more than hearing what our daughters are saying. Learning their emotional language in the absence of words is as vitally important. Watch for little changes in their responses. They may have shorter replies, fewer words to contribute, or a distance in their connection.

These may seem inconsequential, but little signs can be clues to bigger concerns. For example, silence can show a lack of connection; they may be spending more time on devices to fulfilling their "social" quotas. There may be something bothering them, or they may be feeling disconnected, and they don't know why. These are the little things we shouldn't ignore.

You know the spark that lights them up, and what brings them to life. See if you can reignite their love language by pointing out the aspects of it that speak to their hearts. Remind them of their smile and how you miss it. Give them a hug and hold on longer. Write them a note and share the words you haven't been able to exchange. Ask them something other than, "Are you okay?" Try, "You can talk to me whenever you need to. I am in your corner and will be here when you need me."

Notice the little things.

Say the little things.

Do the little things.

Let It Go

When our daughters are small, all the little things may add up and it would be easy to feel the overwhelm. When my daughters were little, I decided to show up and pick the one thing I could do each day that would show them my love in action. Would there be moments I failed to notice, or words

I forgot to say, or things I should have done? Sure! But those things matter, and they tuck those memories away forever. But as our girls get older, all those little things add up and become big life moments—some, we may not get right or we may miss altogether; and in some, we might be the hero. Don't despair. Your teen daughters just want to know that you are always there. But going into those years with the foreknowledge that you might not be the hero of her story anymore will help soften the disappointment for you both when you fail to show up for every little thing. In fact, just focus on the big things because that is what your teens will remember.

This section is going to be hard to read. Your daughters are 90 percent unaware that their actions and words have a 100 percent forceable impact on you. You feel everything they do, say, and go through with your entire being. That's what makes you an amazing mom. But let's be honest. There will be days when your daughters' actions and words will sting. Your daughters know you just as well as you know them. They realize after the fact that they made you sad or that their lack of planning affected you; they learn what your triggers are. It's impossible for two or more females to live in the same house and not know these things about one another. The difference is, since you are the grown-up, you have learned discretion and self-control, and (hopefully) you think before you speak or act.

Our daughters' mood swings, selfishness, or lack of gratefulness are not personal. So, we need to: Let it go. Don't excuse the behavior, but remember there is a season of immaturity, even for the young girl who is trying to live for Jesus. Immaturity doesn't excuse disrespect, but we should remember that they will have their ups and downs regardless, and it is up to us how far we allow those unpredictable moods to affect us and others. Your daughter doesn't know you were up all night sick or with the baby when she asks why you can't take her ice skating for the hundredth time. Even when you give her a reason, she cannot let it go because she isn't thinking about you right now. She is thinking about her friends and the cute Instagram pictures she wants to take. You can't believe how selfish she is, even when you tell her how tired you are. Don't tell her again. You can work on her selfishness later. You both need to let it go. Life lessons and corrections will always be around the corner. Trust me, this never ends. Life gives us enough to handle; we don't need to hold on to hurt for the lessons still being taught. Someday, all the intentional little things will add up, and she will remember the most important thing: Her mom was always there.

A MOTHER'S REFLECTIONS

- How do I love my daughter in the little things?
- Do I tell her I love her, or do I hope my actions will speak those words?
- Do I have trouble letting things go and try to make everything a teaching moment?

WHAT'S A GIRL MOM TO DO

- There is no limit on how much you love your daughter. Love her the way she needs to be loved.
- Identify the most valuable resource you have that would mean the most to her. This could be your time, attention, words, etc.

- Tell her "I love you," even when it feels corny, untimed, or mushy. She still needs to hear those words.

- Let go of the moments of conflict that might cause you to hurt, especially if your daughter hasn't intended to hurt you.

A MOTHER'S PRAYER

Lord, You know I often feel stretched thin, bearing the weight of everyone's needs and juggling all the schedules. Help me to embrace the little things and the little moments to show my daughters a love that would do anything for them. Please give me wisdom to discern when to correct and when to comfort. Help me to show kindness in the ways I teach her, and grace when I need to forgive. Give me good rest and strength to enter each new day with new mercies. Thank You for the gift of raising daughters. In Jesus' name, Amen.

5

An Invitation to Friendship

I HAVE LEARNED THAT THERE are two welcome and open invitations into the hearts of our girls. First, there will be times when they ask for our help and comfort. When they extend this invitation, we should step gently into their space and help them navigate their feelings. We can ask good questions, share words of comfort, and encourage them to think ahead. The second invitation will be unspoken and unannounced. Cues we will notice include their quiet demeanor and inward processing, longing for connection. This invitation gives us permission to quietly step into sacred conversations, where their hearts are questioning big life problems or matters of the heart. They cannot quite pinpoint what is on their mind, until you give them the space to be present with them.

Our immediate reaction when either invitation arrives is to rush right in. This delicate (and confusing) balance between respecting our daughter's space and privacy while being present and available is a challenge to maintain. As our girls enter the teen years, we learn their heart language. We study their body language. We learn the cues and the patterns of their communication. From the time they are little girls, they are watching how we speak and how we feel. They begin to create their own language of communicating with us. We learn to read between the lines, and we become an expert in knowing what they need and when.

Becoming a good friend to our older daughters means we step in and step out of their personal space with respect to their heart. We know when to listen and when to speak. We know the cues by paying attention. We learn how they think and teach them how to navigate their emotions in a healthy and biblical way. Sure, we don't sacrifice our own feelings on the altar of effort, but the heart is a delicate matter, and often, our daughters just need to know we are available, without needing intervention.

Be available and walk tenderly. Your own heart may speak a whole different language than your daughter's. Take time to evaluate if your advice or comfort is coming from "protector mode" or from truth and true encouragement. Often, our desire to protect them can get in the way of helping our girls, maybe hindering how they handle and process hard situations.

Learn to listen to the unspoken words of your daughters' hearts. It is there you will find the deepest well of connection.

"What's wrong?"

"Nothing."

"Are you sure? I know you, and you seem quiet today. Do you want to talk?"

"I'm fine."

Cue the tears. Then the hug, mixed with more tears and healing.

Perhaps this conversation sounds familiar. I've lived this scenario on repeat over the last three decades of raising daughters, and it never gets easier. This is the "language" of daughters. The words we say matter. Mothers learn to read between the lines, listening to what daughters say and what they don't say. We watch for signals of concern and give them the tools to have good and helpful conversations. We learn to see the innermost thoughts and feelings of our girls and draw the pieces out that are hurting, confused, and struggling. We also rejoice with them over victories, celebrations, and small wins.

Even when we feel disconnected or far away from our daughters, we know their hearts better than anyone. Matters of the heart should be handled with care; we would want the same for ourselves. The biggest conundrum we will face is how to protect our daughters, without micromanaging them. Should we intervene with their relationships? How can we guide them through deep waters? When do we give our opinions and when do we hold back? Should we step in and help, or let them fall, stand back up, and be brave?

Some of us had mothers who emotionally walked in and out of our lives. Relationships are not all perfect, and while we unfold a growing connection in the relationships with our own daughters, we must also acknowledge the worth of the work it will take for us all. I understand that not all mother-daughter relationships will be good, positive, or perfect. There will be women who read this book and experience profound sadness or anger. I want this chapter to speak to the imperfect, broken, and hard relationships that exist. I don't want to sugarcoat this reality with a strong emphasis on a glamorous mother-daughter relationship when some of us sit in broken, hard places.

As we raise daughters, let us learn how to avoid the pitfalls that can turn friends into foes—not hiding from the past, but living in the reality of today and staying hopeful for the future.

My Way or the Highway

For those who have been raised in a household with a controlling or otherwise difficult mother, be careful not to repeat those unhealthy patterns. You cannot bully your daughter into a relationship with you. If you tend toward control over her behavior, her wardrobe, her friends, and her choices, you will be surprised to discover that when your daughter can leave home, she will leave the circle of your control.

As harsh as this sounds, we all do this a little (or a lot). Control does two things. It pushes people away; it leans in too hard to engage in a relationship with unrealistic expectations and attempts to micromanage every detail in the other person's life, including their behavior. You will also recognize control as harsh responses when you are annoyed with your daughter's inability to achieve a standard you have set. Or you might become impatient and step in to take over when things don't go your way.

Perhaps you have been in a relationship where guilt became a motivator for connection. Guilt begets guilt. When we become desperate for control, or feel we are losing our grasp on the decisions our daughters make, we may use guilt to manipulate their relationship with us. What may feel genuine and real will eventually disintegrate and not last.

Instead, a long-lasting relationship with your daughter will require humility and honesty. Your commitment to meeting her in the middle, showing deference when she makes choices you don't agree with, and being there when she needs you, creates a genuine and lifelong relationship. Your heart may get hurt. Your toes may get stepped on, and someday you will not have first place in her life. Learning how to hold your daughter in a tender embrace, with a loose grip of control, begins when she is small. How can you let go when the time comes if your grip is so tight she cannot breathe? Moms, you will have a connection with your daughter that can never be broken. Every day, every year, loosen your control and micromanagement of every piece of your daughter's life. Someday, that cord of love can reach across distances and your heart will always feel the tug of her needs. She needs you to be available, so when the day comes, and she needs you the most, you are still there, ready to love well.

When God gave you a daughter, He also gave you a friend. He also gave you a heart to be a mother and friend. And he has given us the best examples and the fruits of the Spirit—like love, patience, self-control, and kindness—to guide us in both motherhood and friendship. God loves us as His children, but He doesn't over-parent us. And He is also our greatest friend.

Can We Be Friends?

Our main role is "mother" during the formative years of our daughters' lives. This transition to friends isn't easy or natural to everyone. It will take time and consistent engagement for your daughters to see you as a woman living your own life. Our daughters don't really see us as "fellow women" with our own friends, struggles, work, routines, and all the things they themselves are managing to balance as well. We have always been Mom, the one who nurtures, helps, and is always there. Our hard-earned moments with friends, time for exercise, hospitality, ministry, and date nights with our spouse are all unobserved by them until they begin to see us as friends and not just Mom.

I discovered this to be true when my girls were in their mid-to-late twenties. Becoming friends with your daughters will require a new dance. Be honest and let them see your struggles. Ask them to pray for you. Talk about the things that are outside of what you want to do for them and what they need from you. You will learn to honor one another's schedules. Your discussions will become more about life, and your role as teacher will become less talk and more example. Your daughter will always see you as her mother, but your example to her of a healthy friendship will help you both navigate this new season.

It is no surprise that your daughters will change as they grow. Their hearts will always be knit to yours, but over time, our girls grow up to be women. Their interests evolve, and they spread their wings beyond the circle of your family. This is a beautiful process. Enjoy every minute! The most surprising part of an evolving relationship with your daughter is the moment you realize it's not just the two of you in this big world of relationships. Her world widens beyond the most singular and impactful relationship she may ever have—her relationship with you.

As her world broadens, everything about your relationship will begin to change. She doesn't think of you first when she is planning her social calendar. You may not be her first call when she needs someone to talk to. When her time is spread thin, you are still there on the sidelines, cheering her on. When we pray for our daughters to have good friends, we should be prepared and thankful for the day that God answers this prayer. He will send new and trusted friends, who look out for our daughters' hearts. Be careful not to feel like someone has stepped on your toes. There are seasons in your mother-daughter relationship when you will be second. Taking second place doesn't mean you are not important to her. She still loves you and needs you.

How do we communicate caution or concern when a friend might just cheer them on? Can we bring the fun, or will we always be thinking about their safety and well-being? Will we always be learning how to simultaneously juggle our needs, their needs, and our friendship? It is possible, but it takes work. Isn't that what a good friend is willing to do? She speaks the truth in love, always wanting the best for her friend. She can forgive when asked, embrace growth, celebrate surprises, and be present when life is tough. I think the word "friend" should be added to the thesaurus right next to the word "mother."

From the beginning, your job is to prepare her to be independent, strong, and kind. She will make new friends and find her people. These are exciting milestones, where we navigate teaching and supporting, yet stepping away without the need to be "needed." To help navigate your feelings as this change occurs, make a mental checklist of those areas in which you are feeling isolated or left out. Ask yourself, "Are her choices reflecting the valuable lessons I have been instilling in her?" "Does she need my guidance to navigate her decisions?" You will remain her trusted support system, her trusted back-up to lean on when other friends disappear or move away. You are steadfast to the end.

Raising daughters is personal. Yet, we should be careful not to take everything personally. Our goal is to see our daughters live their best life, and when we make ourselves the center of the story, we get in the way of allowing Christ to do His work in their lives. It really isn't about us. There are seeds of friendship we plant in the years we are raising them. We spend countless hours teaching, laughing, and wiping their tears. We are the first face they see when they wake up, and the last before they go to sleep at night. But the day comes when we are on the sidelines texting "Good morning," "How are you today?" or "I am proud of you" and not getting an immediate reply. Does this mean we aren't important to them? We are now among the many people and pursuits our daughters are juggling themselves. Let's be careful not to feel overlooked. The sidelines remove us from the spotlight. We are still on the same team, just not front and center.

Your feelings are real and will sting the first few times you experience them. You may find out news about her life from someone else first, and you may hear your daughter say, "Oh, didn't I tell you?" She may plan events with others and not invite you. Not because she was purposefully leaving you out, but perhaps because this is what you taught her to do—find a community, make good friends, show hospitality, bear one another's burdens, and take care of herself, her family, and her relationship with the Lord. No one ever told us that when we prepare our daughters to create a successful, thriving life that we wouldn't be at the center of it all. We go from teacher and helper to seemingly forgotten or only "on call" when needed. You will always be her mother. If you want to be her friend, treat her like one. Give her the space you would to another friend, finding the rhythm that works the best for both of you. With seven daughters and two daughters-in-love, I have nine unique mother-daughter friendships I engage with on different levels daily.

Be your daughter's friend. Go for it. I don't know what I would do without my daughters in my daily life. Raising them was a joy, but now that they are grown women, living their own lives, I have a unique friendship with each one. They still need me as their mom. That never changed. But we work hard at the pieces of our lives that have shaped us to be good friends. The best friendships are a give and take, a love and learning. Our friendships are unique from other relationships in that moms never stop "mothering."

Habits We Should Pay Attention To

I would be remiss to not talk about the very habits we struggle to put away as our friendships with our daughters evolve, which can threaten our relationship with them as a whole. I have listed them below, to give us a place of reference if we are feeling tension, we cannot put our finger on.

1. Control your tongue. What we say and how we say it is vital in any friendship. You might have to change the way you speak to your daughter once they hit their late teens and early twenties. It is not your job to teach her something or correct her every time you disagree. Give advice when asked or are given permission. When you spend time together, don't make the conversation all about you. Consider what you say, how you say it, and who you are talking to.
2. Demands are guilt-driven actions. This would look and sound like, "I haven't seen you in a long time." "Why don't you reach out to me more?" " I did x, y, z for you; the least you could do is call or text me." "I put you through college; I don't think finding time for a cup of coffee with me would be too much."

3. Control is a sneaky habit. We might use words like: "They need my help. They have no idea what they are doing. They need to fix this, or I will do this for them."
4. Interference will send you to the sidelines quickly. Stay out of their business unless it is your business, or a health, safety, or emergency situation. Learn to ask questions the right way. Engage regularly, and not just when you want to be nosy or involved.
5. Privacy is key. Keep your daughters' conversations and business private. You don't need to tell your other friends or interfere where she needs space and time.
6. Apologize when needed. Don't let time pass on misunderstandings or conflicts. Say you're sorry and learn from your mistakes. Remember, you are the older of the two and should know what a healthy friendship looks like by now. You will always be knit to your daughter's heart. You know when she is happy or when she hurts. All she needs to do is follow that invisible heartstring back to you, and you will be there, waiting. A good friend always waits, no matter what.
7. Give her space. In other words, follow her lead. If she reaches out to call or message every day, follow her lead. Don't show up unannounced too many times. Sometimes, the sweetest surprises follow a spontaneous visit, but we should be careful to consider her space, schedule, and time.

In general, girls are creatures of communication. Words are important, which means there are a lot of words in our home. There can be so much talking, my ears literally hurt by the end of the day. Most of my time is spent listening and talking to my daughters. With seven girls, there are so many words exchanged. I find myself losing my grip on patience, kindness, and correcting attitudes. Small things can be monumental, and we can lose the ability to hear ourselves. No one is exempt from losing track of what is important. Regardless of how much you love one another, there will be moments when you both make mistakes. Your words might cut deep. Your actions will be selfish. Humility and self-awareness are two of the greatest gifts mothers and daughters can give one another—all encompassed in two "little" words that have so much life-giving power in this world:

"I'm sorry."

Oh, the love it takes to turn a conflict around. The humility it takes to admit how everything went all wrong when it didn't need to. It will take self-reflection and awareness to know our personal triggers, to control our tongues, and to use them wisely when we need to make things right. Telling someone you're sorry isn't easy. It doesn't always mean your words didn't have "some truth," or your actions didn't come from a place of hurt. I'm sorry means restoration. It's the selfless act of showing up and being present. Mothers and daughters alike can heal a long line of past hurts and painful moments when they reflect on Christ's command to love one another: "Just as I have loved you, you also are to love one another." (John 13:34) When words are many, let those two words be comfortable on your lips. What an example to our girls to show the humble act of returning hurt with healing. Be the first to initiate this act of love and friendship. You are an adult, so lead by example.

Your daughters will make you laugh until you are rolling on the floor, while trying not to pee your pants. You will laugh until you cry. You will annoy them, and they will make your life complicated and amazing, all at the same time. You will argue and disagree about things. You will grab coffee and go thrifting together. There will be weeks when you speak to one another every day, and other times when you will have to check in on her to be sure she is okay. Sometimes, it will be personal, and you will both have to reach into the deep recesses of your hearts to fix something that might be wrong. There may not always be something you can fix or make better. You will exchange recipes, make one another meals, care for one another when sick, and share tears and celebrations. Every season will look different, but the bottom line is that it will take two. You may be so different, that people wonder how you can be related. Your similarities can bond you or break you. It is up to you.

Someone will replace you someday. They will steal your daughter's heart, give them a new home, and trade your help for theirs. Dear mama, no one else could ever be their mother. No one will ever love like you love your daughter. I share this to remind you that it might be easy to feel pushed out, left out, ignored, or even disliked at some stage of your daughter's "growing up years," but between the time they are little girls and you hand the baton of independence over to them, protect your relationship at all cost. There will be outside opinions, voices, and influences that try to replace your role as mentor, helper, listener, and comforter. We don't have to believe the lie that we are not important. Without strong-arming control over your daughter's life, be careful not to micromanage her and dictate her decisions, but hold loosely to the outcome, with everything you have. Tread lightly, invest deeply, love fiercely. Above all, live what you teach. Your voice matters. Make every moment matter.

Mothers love fiercely, unselfishly, and unequivocally. It takes two. Don't let anything get in the way. *Mothers, love every day like it is your last.*

A MOTHER'S REFLECTIONS

- As I look to the future, which areas might I struggle with "letting go" of the most?
- How can I practice being a good friend and mother right now?

WHAT'S A GIRL MOM TO DO?

- I will focus on areas like trust, wisdom, discernment, and discretion in my own life, so when my daughters are grown, I can model the best example of friendship.
- I will practice the slow release of their time and attention while I can.

A MOTHER'S PRAYER

Father, You have shown me what it means to be a good friend. Please lead my daughter into good and godly friendships as she grows. When You gave me a daughter, You gave me a best friend. Help me to remember she is Yours first, and guide me through this new season of adding "friend" to my role as "mother." Thank You for modeling parental love and friendship

to me. Even when I feel I deserve more time and attention, draw me back to You. Thank You for working in our lives to establish such a beautiful built-in relationship.
In Jesus' name, Amen.

6

Girl Talk

MANY OF US COME FROM a generation where there were gaping holes in conversations about our femininity, stewardship, our appearance, self-care, or style. The list of topics our own mothers never talked to us about has left us scrambling for answers. We've become so afraid of our own femininity that we feel awkward or wrong talking to our girls about the most personal and private matters someone should be talking to them about. That someone should be you. Now is always the best moment to set aside time for some girl talk. Our culture today is confused by true femininity, and our daughters need someone with a healthy view of the bodies God gave them, and how our womanhood is a gift from God.

Moms, don't let your fears force your daughters to explore or find someone else to talk to them about their bodies. Our job as mothers to daughters is to guide our girls through the transitions their bodies will go through as they get older. If you've done the hard work of honest conversations, beginning when they are little, then the bigger topics won't seem as awkward when our daughters are preteens and teens. Our daughters follow our cues. The time and the tone we bring to these conversations will set the trajectory for ongoing conversations in their growing up years. Our goal is to break the cycle of shame and discomfort women often experience when we think about our bodies. The comfort level you have with your own womanhood, and the approach you take when talking to your daughters, will influence their personal views for the future.

When we choose to leave the questions unanswered and the topics unaddressed, we send a message of shame. Take time to consider how you may not have been prepared or taught to embrace your femininity, or how to care for your body. What would you have wanted to be different for yourself? I'd encourage you to smile and relax, knowing that some things will be shocking to your girls when you talk to them. Don't let that scare you away from the conversations. They will thank you down the road for giving them a wholesome and wholehearted, upfront talk to the very things that make them a woman.

Femininity has become a taboo word. Will we be the generation of mothers brave enough to tell our daughters that they are beautiful designs and uniquely God's masterpiece? Do we even remember what it means to be a woman who can give God the glory with her beauty and still be different from everyone else? Do we "cancel" the beauty of womanhood until we aren't able to define what it means to be feminine? In a culture where the pendulum swings wide with ultra-modest conservative views of beauty to the world that has almost all but eradicated the difference between man and woman, let us be the mothers who remind the world what it means to be a woman of God, designed to give Him glory and to bear His image.

Femininity is unique to every girl. And thank goodness, because if the entire population of women looked and acted like me, we might have a boring world. When our daughters look in the mirror, what do we want them to see? What will they believe about themselves? How will they steward and care for their bodies, minds, and souls—all of which make us complete women. When others see us, what do they see? What will they know of Christ? I have found that many of us struggle to have conversations involving these good and hefty questions.

With seven daughters sharing a bathroom, the drawers (and the drains) were filled with hair ties and clips, curlers, straighteners, and brushes. One might think that hair would be the least of my worries. In the grand scheme of things, hair care was a small part of the role given to me as "self-care manager" when I became a mom to many daughters. Don't get me wrong. There is an age of awareness and independence that strikes around thirteen, but anything before that magical age is a downright repetitive monologue, every single day. "Did you brush your hair?" "You can't find your brush?" "Where could it have gone?" "When was the last time you washed your hair?" The simplest of tasks become a daily lesson in self-care for our girls. Our reminders to care for everything from brushing hair to brushing teeth should come from a place of encouraging healthy habits. Be careful not to create an environment where your daughter becomes obsessive or self-conscious of her appearance.

Helping our girls develop healthy daily habits when they are little become just that, healthy daily habits. These practices are not drudgery or vanity, but part of a daily routine. Start now; you can never begin too early. Teach your daughters the importance of self-care, which leads to stewardship of their bodies. While the world shouts conflicting and unbiblical messages about identity and body image, we must communicate a wholesome and positive message to combat what our daughters are hearing.

The struggle to stay on top of every little detail can take time, and so the words "self-care" are exactly what we strive to equip our daughters to do. We want them to care for themselves, but the transition is tricky. How do we hand the baton of care over to them without micromanaging every little detail? Stewardship of our bodies is vital to our womanhood. We may not have been given the gift of intentional motherhood when we were young ourselves, but the invaluable insight and investment into your daughter's life in this area will be something that lasts a lifetime.

Talk to your daughters about the amazing gift of womanhood we have been given by God, our Creator, reminding them how important it is to learn to listen to our bodies. We want our daughters to embrace the body and mind God has given them and steward their lives to the best of their ability. From what we eat, how we spend our time, to how we model true rest, God will use our bodies and minds if we are willing.

Don't let fear dictate your conversations or example when raising your girls. We may worry we won't do it all the right way and overcompensate with micromanaging and fear-based conversations. Or we may swing wide in the other direction and carry on the age-old tradition that some generations never talked about these things, and we turned out "just fine."

Giving our girls the gift of honest conversations, a wholesome outlook on their femininity, and a well-balanced plan of stewarding our future is one of the biggest gifts we can give them. The message that reminds them that they are beautiful, inside and out. God's design is perfect.

Discovering Her Style

My mom loved makeup, nail polish, glitter, perfume, and bright colors. I am pretty sure she didn't know what to do with me. I never took a liking to makeup. I couldn't bear the thought of nail polish on my fingers. I was drawn to earth tones and still have an aversion to glitter and strongly scented perfumes. So, how does a mom parent a daughter with such a different style? Do we try to win our girls over to our own preferences? In today's culture, it is important to note the value of fostering a culture of femininity in our homes. While drawing on our daughter's input, we can guide them with their own style in mind. It takes great intention and time. How do we help them navigate their own preferences without squashing their spirit and creativity? These are common areas we all encounter while raising daughters, and while there isn't a one-size-fits-all answer, some basic guidelines have helped me navigate our way through.

As a plain Jane kind of girl, I never cared much for bright colors, high heels, or jewelry either. Don't get me wrong. I think it is absolutely fabulous to see other women lean into their unique style and show an amazing ability to dress up or down with such finesse. I don't have an aversion or conviction that keeps me from desiring to be more stylish. I haven't settled for less or desired to become more. I am content with my neutral wardrobe, splashed with soft undertones. I didn't wear makeup until I was in my thirties, and I always felt out of place in my clothing. It took me that long to know exactly who I was in the world of women, shopping in stores where glam and style were the fad, and online Instagram styling accounts didn't exist or normalize my style. It took time for me to feel comfortable in my own skin, and the confidence to say, "This is me."

Raising daughters who know more about themselves and their bodies at a young age allows them to feel confident in what they wear and how to communicate their unique style. Among my seven very different daughters, the style choices have been all over the map; but I have been able to see and accept where they were leaning and have guided them in navigating their choices. When we go shopping, I ask questions about what they like, and why. I give them the chance to think about their preferences. This is often overlooked. How will they know if they've never had to think about it? Some of my girls had a style preference and could communicate this to me from an early age. For other daughters, it took a few years of frustrating shopping trips and helping them narrow down their personal style choices. You may not think this would be such a vital topic, but the lessons learned over tears and frustration with a few of my girls reminded me that not all mothers and daughters know how to navigate moments like these.

We go from picking out the cutest clothes when our girls are little to a notable transition: the day they have "nothing to wear." To us, their wardrobe seems adequate, and our budget doesn't allow for an entire overhaul for the sake of style. Other girls don't know their style, let alone care about shopping or what they wear. As a mom, being prepared ahead with good questions and shopping together (and shopping sales!) will allow our daughters to begin discovering and owning their style and making wise choices. Listed here are questions and conversation starters that will help you help your daughters to navigate style and the shopping experience in the years to come.

Conversation Starters

- Your style is an extension of who you are.
- You can gain confidence from knowing your style and what you are comfortable in. You don't have to feel overwhelmed.
- You are learning a life skill of budgeting in style.
- You may change your preferences in your clothing and style choices over time, and that is okay.
- Modesty and style can go hand in hand. Learning how to dress in a way that expresses your personality and aligns with your values is a skill you can and will develop.

Questions to Guide the Conversation

- What do you feel the most comfortable wearing and why?
- What colors and patterns make you feel the most like yourself?
- How do you want your clothing to represent who you are?
- What do you like about your current clothing and wardrobe, and what do you think is missing?
- How can we shop smart, and how does this give us more options in our spending and our choices?

Stewarding Your Body

If you're in the thick of raising little girls, it is hard to imagine the day when your daughter will not like the outfit you picked out for her. There will soon be a day when she doesn't want you to braid or brush her hair, and the next thing you know, the top items on her Christmas list are a straightener, heat protectant, and a gift card for highlights at the salon. It happens that fast. It is gloriously frustrating, then freeing, and then you are standing behind her in the mirror, adjusting her veil on her wedding day, and you think, "How did this happen?"

We can miss the transition because it happens in the days and hours of letting go and holding on. A tug-of-war so fierce it far surpasses working through the knots in her hair. Our goal is to prepare them with good self-care habits, knowledge of their bodies, and how to steward their health.

Taking a hands-off approach would be the easier route, and sadly, many moms give up because they think their girls will figure it out on their own someday. But don't take your daughter's pushback, laziness, and lackadaisical efforts too personally. This is where being a mom to daughters stretches us to think beyond the emotions of the moment and know that one day, all our efforts to teach them how to steward their lives will be worth it. Sometimes, it is easier to just do everything for them. We can avoid their attitudes and arguments, and our relentless follow up to be sure they are stewarding their lives well.

Stewardship is a broad stroke word for teaching our daughters how to live independently from us. But really, it is so much more. Stewardship encapsulates honoring the femininity, health, and gifts God has given us. Once my girls became more independent, we sat down together at the beginning of the year and each made a short list of areas where we could steward our lives better. We focused on our physical, emotional, and spiritual areas first.

Examples of notes they made for themselves under these categories included:

PHYSICAL	EMOTIONAL	SPIRITUAL
• Get in 10,000 steps a day • Minimize my screen time • Drink more water • Smile more • Try a new haircut • Clean out my closet/store seasonal clothes/donate the rest	• Be more open to suggestions from others • Talk to Mom or Dad about my problems or ask for help • Spend more time outside • Meet up with friends and get out of the house more	• Read my Bible more • Remove distractions that take my time away from personal time with God • Study more of God's character and who He is to me daily • Take my cares to God before I turn to social media for support or validation outside of His truth

I have saved quite a few of their lists from over the years because it is exciting and rewarding for them to see their growth. Most of all, I want them to know I am and always will be in their corner.

Holy Hormones

Cue the tears and exaggerated eye rolls. Be prepared for the mood changes and the sullen behavior. It seems like overnight, our daughters aren't our little girls anymore. Just yesterday, she wanted to spend time with me but now would rather be with her friends. Where are the tears coming from? What did I do wrong this time? Why the eye roll? Where did her new insecurity come from? Where has my little girl gone?

Let's not call this a "bad phase." Can we just say it is hard and tricky to navigate? Imagine having eight women in your home at the same time. That was my life for many years, and there were days when no one wanted to be my friend, and I couldn't say or do anything right. It wasn't bad, but it surely wasn't pretty at times. I realized quickly that I had to be the one to tell those holy hormones (God did give them to us, praise Him) who was in control of the tone of our home. I taught my girls early on that our hormones don't control us. That conversation didn't always fly, but it was a good standard that helped keep us all level-headed and self-aware of what was really going on when everything felt wrong.

Hormones can get a bad rap. I get it, they change how we think, feel, and are sometimes relentless. Our emotions can be up, and then down, and sometimes all over the place; but if we talk about hormones and how they affect our bodies, then maybe we can better understand the amazing bodies God created. Talk about hormones with your girls. As my daughters reached their pre-teen years, I began to explain the intricate design of our bodies and how their hormones are working for them. They learned to track their cycles, paying attention to how they were feeling and what could be causing their highs and lows each week. It was an important part of understanding how God made their bodies uniquely, and therefore, not growing annoyed or despising all of the changes happening as they grew older.

Understanding what hormones are and what their functions are in a girl's body can be a fascinating topic of discussion. Our hormones are what make us female. Study and learn how to recognize the impact our hormones are having on our bodies and how to recognize when something isn't right. Learning how God made our bodies to function is foundational to these conversations with our girls. Don't skip over this topic. Nothing else will make sense to your daughters if you do. Tell them about progesterone, estrogen, testosterone. Provide them with the science and reliable, godly sources. Explain the impact on their emotions and body responses. Allow them to ask questions and give them the tools to identify what their body is doing and when. Hormones don't have to control us.

Stay current with your girls about how they are feeling, emotionally and physically. Remind your daughters that when "they just don't feel like themselves" there is usually a reason, and most of the time, there is something they can do about it—even if that means a shoulder to cry on or a friend to laugh and eat chocolate with you. Be their friend. That is what you would want, and most likely wished you'd had. Whatever you do, don't take their moodiness or outbursts personally. It's not about you, even though it sure feels like it. Those holy hormones can shake things up for everyone; but in the end, we love our daughters through the journey.

"The Talk"

While my girls changed into their cozy jammies, I set up the few special snacks I had packed for our weekend away. I had reserved a special girls' getaway, planned activities, and prepared my heart and mind for the conversations we would have. When my first daughter was twelve, we took this girls' weekend alone. But, as the Lord added more girls to our family, we would all go every time the next daughter in the line-up of girls turned twelve.

I chose the first evening to get into the heavier topics. I did this deliberately to give my girls the remainder of the weekend to work through their questions and process somewhat shocking and new information. My girls had not had previous conversations about sex, and this weekend away was planned for this specific purpose. Building a relationship of trust before you hit go on the big talks is so important.

Our hours cycled through light-hearted talks about our favorite things, our dreams, plans, boys, and friends, and we gradually made our way into the big stuff…sex, purity, babies, marriage, boyfriends, intimacy, and whatever other questions they had. Did they all receive and handle these conversations well? I would say no. Imagine seven different personalities, from private to personable, from slow processors to extroverted verbal communicators. From my point of view, the interactions were amusing and serious at the same time. There were moments when I could barely keep a straight face, and others when I had to take one-on-one time with them.

With three different sets of girls born in three different decades, the "girl talk" weekends have looked different each time. Regardless of who was on the receiving end of this special girls' talk, all my daughters over twelve joined in every time. The younger girls looked up to their older sisters, and to be quite honest, the older girls set a more relaxed tone and added some great advice to each conversation we had.

Our weekends were never a one and done talk. I'll never forget the different reactions to each of our conversations about their body changes, puberty, and sex. Each daughter reacted differently to our discussions. As I carefully laid out the details of how our bodies were created so uniquely and purposefully, I could see their minds begin to register the concept of purpose beyond their limited knowledge and curiosity began to set in. By the time our talk had reached the topic of intercourse, they grew silent. One of my daughters left the room, locking herself in the bathroom. Another grabbed her notebooks and pen and began peppering me with questions. Another sat with her eyes and mouth gaping, in complete shock. Two of my girls had their eyes closed and hands over their mouths, exclaiming, "Ewwwwwww!"

After each conversation at our various girl talk getaways, I gave them time to recalibrate. I calmly told them I would give them every opportunity to ask me questions, and we'd have time to talk more. I learned that in that specific moment, it was important for me to keep talking assuredly, chuckling with them, acknowledging their mortification, and remarking and focusing on how there is so much beauty to sex and how they couldn't fully understand that until they were married, and I didn't expect them to.

Moms, the tone and setting of discussions like this are 100 percent up to you. Work hard to put your daughters at ease; give them a safe space for their reactions in real time. Be careful not to tease them or allow shame to enter the room. The goal is for them to trust you with the handling of these important topics. Don't wait until someone else has told them "the facts" without a biblical view and a wholesome, trusted approach to their femininity. You may have experienced the sex education talk like I did. When I turned twelve, I was handed an encyclopedia with the "sex" page bookmarked and told to read it. That was my education; no discussion with my mother followed. Two weeks before I was to be married, she asked if I had any questions about "you know." Of course, I simply said no.

Give your daughters the gift of trust and time. You will never regret this intentional decision. Did I just whisk away my girls for a weekend and blast them with hours of information overload? Definitely not.

I always precipitate the big weekend talk with years of specific and timely discussions. In the years and days prior to our weekends away, I present them each with a special "welcome to womanhood" box filled with special items such as: deodorant, pads, tampons, a journal, special pens, chocolate, electrolytes, face wash, a razor, shaving cream, a few makeup items, a loofah in their favorite color, shower gel, a handwritten note, and a small carry case for personal items to be stored and carried to and from school, youth group, etc. Before giving them this box, we chat about what changes their bodies might be experiencing soon. By that time, we have already transitioned from the "training bra stage" to a real bra and have had discussions about their appearance and their awareness of what is happening to their bodies.

In fact, they all anxiously awaited their "special box" because each has witnessed their older sisters receive the same, and they've seen the experience as something wholesome and something to look forward to. By the time we head to our weekend getaway, they have had stepping stones to important conversations, and we have been building a relationship of trust. As prepared as I ever am for our weekends away, I know their reactions may differ, and I pray the Lord will help me to remain sensitive to how my girls process new and personal information so differently.

Moms, you should be the first and most important voice to your girls in the conversations and her ideas about her growing and changing body. If you feel uncomfortable or don't know what to say, it is time to get comfortable with your own skin and give her a safe and wholesome outlook on her body and femininity. Whatever you fail to talk to her about, she will search for and discover another way. With social media, peers with different worldviews, and a search bar just one click away, your daughter can be exposed to so many conflicting messages about her body and what to expect.

Think about how you first heard about your period and how you were or weren't prepared. Did you have more questions than answers? Did your body changes feel shameful or cause you embarrassment? Did you feel prepared for what changes you experienced over the years? Did you feel comfortable talking to your mom about your feelings and asking questions you might have had? The culture has made all these things so open as to no longer be special or sacred. Our girls deserve more. We can change how our daughters feel about this topic just by talking to them candidly, being truthful, and preparing them. Will it be awkward? Yes. As comfortable as we may become in sharing details with them, their first impressions will be shock, concern, and awkwardness. But the great news is that our delivery, our responses, and our answers can help them reach a maturity in knowing about their bodies and learning to embrace how God made women. We can normalize the once awkward topics that have been avoided by moms for decades.

Below is a helpful list of topics and talking points to help you navigate these important topics with your daughters.

1. Practice talking to your little girls about their bodies with a wholesome tone and positive words. Affirm modesty and privacy, yet be careful not to let shame be part of your conversations. It would be easy for girls to confuse modesty with shame when we discuss those two topics.

2. Watch for symptoms of mood changes, fatigue, headaches, changes in their breast or pubic areas. Acknowledge their emotional changes and give space for tears and outbursts. Help them to be aware and understand what is really going on inside their bodies to cause these changes. Help them identify their internal feelings ahead of time, so they are able to navigate their actions.
3. Help them transition from camisoles or tee tanks to padded training bras to avoid teasing and embarrassment with peers or in social settings. Take note that this is a very sensitive and sometimes awkward time for our young daughters. They become very self-conscious for the first time, and our calm and loving words and attitudes will make a big difference in their comfort levels when wearing their new undergarments for the first time. This is a great opportunity to begin the modesty discussion.
4. Begin planning your special box or gift for your daughters. Once their bodies begin to show any changes, their period will be within one to two years or less from this time. Have the "period and other details" talk before they start menstruating. Every mom chooses a different time for this talk. I chose to have this talk once I noticed body hair, and my daughter began to ask me questions about these changes. I wanted them to be prepared, not afraid and know what to expect when the time came. We would talk about shaving, and I would give them a shaving "tutorial." I also showed them how to use a pad and maintain cleanliness.

5. Your big talk should happen as early as you know or feel that your daughters will be exposed to peer conversations and circles where this might come up. In our home, the timing was later, but I have friends who wanted to preempt peer groups talks. Another time sensitive deciding factor would be if your daughter is asking questions or may have been accidentally exposed to material you hadn't approved. Know your daughter and you will know the right time.
6. Don't end the conversations after the big talk. There is so much you can and should talk to your daughters about. Don't view the girl talks as a 1, 2, 3 and done. Keep the conversations going. Help them track their cycles and learn about ovulation, hormones, healthy diets, skin care, and more.

A MOTHER'S REFLECTIONS

- Growing and changing isn't easy for any of us. Being a girl or a grown-up woman isn't easy. May I remember how hard, confusing, and sometimes challenging those younger years can be.

WHAT'S A GIRL MOM TO DO?

- Get comfortable with your own body and all the changes both you and your daughters' bodies will experience. Educate yourself so you can help educate your daughters.

- Normalize the conversations that might otherwise be awkward in today's society.

- Be present in the physical and emotional changes to guide your daughters through those times.

- Don't take many things too personally. These challenges will pass. Usually, our daughters' fraught emotions are hormones talking.

- Show compassion and patience. Avoid instilling shame or embarrassment.

- Honor her space and point her back to her Creator and His plan for her life.

A MOTHER'S PRAYER

Lord, thank You for my womanhood. Help me to be compassionate and tender to the changes and surprises that are soon coming for my daughter. I trust You to guide me through our conversations and the emotions to come.
In Jesus' name, Amen.

PART TWO

Her Strong Start

Building Connection That Guides Her Growth

7

Habits to Last a Lifetime

THE MOMENT I HEARD HER yell at her sister, I recognized that voice. It was mine. My daughter was becoming me, or more accurately put, she was picking up my habits—the good and not so good. The Holy Spirit was alive and active in my home because raising girls gives you a front-row seat to all your personal habits. All my sharp edges and the daily habits that hadn't been given much time to soften were now front and center. Every time I heard a raised voice, an impatient tone, or a comment like, "I don't have the time for that right now," a sharp pain of regret and conviction stabbed me. Like I said, the Holy Spirit was giving me ample opportunity to show up, grow up, and to live up to the standards I wanted my daughters to have when they were one day, fully grown women.

I know it is mind-stretching to imagine your toddlers as adults and your teens as your best friend. Trust me, the path forward leads somewhere, and that place is being decided now. There is hope for the yelling mom. There is patience for the weary mom. There is grace for our daughters who are watching us and mimicking us in their habits. Don't be afraid of what is to come. You have time.

We could spend chapters unfolding an exhaustive list of habits involving our households, health, spiritual disciplines, and more. I've decided to focus on a few habits that will guide the rest of our lives and offer opportunity for growth as we become more like Jesus, which is a helpful goal when raising daughters. It is my hope and prayer that this chapter will free you from the weight of perfection and the endless lists and remind you that our daughters will see the growth and sanctification He does in us. Nothing will motivate them more to have a relationship with their Savior than knowing they have a mother who surrenders her life to Him daily.

Our words and our time are the two areas we give the most of to our children. Let's examine our hearts as we focus on how we spend our time. Forming the right habits will last a lifetime.

Our Words

My home has never been quiet. While not the loud, wrestling, tackling, booming "boy" noise we heard when our three sons were still living at home, the noise created by seven girls was a combination of seven shared opinions, seven replies, and seven voices singing, arguing, and talking, all at the same time. Girls talk a lot. It is what they do best. But there is one caveat: Teen girls have so much to say . . . unless their mom is trying to have a conversation with them. Sound familiar? There are times when my girls are talking so much, I lose track of the conversation, as they jump from topic to topic. But the moment I want to engage in a meaningful and intentional conversation with them, it's as if they have forgotten how to talk altogether.

"How was school?"

"Fine."

"Did you have a good day?"

"Yes."

"Are you okay? Is there anything you'd like to talk about?"

"No."

"Did you get to talk to your friends today?"

"Yep."

Engaging conversation, right? This is sometimes how it goes. Sadly, it has become the norm for this generation. I have seen moms give up or think this lack of engagement is normal. They slowly surrender their voices and their influence of their daughters to other people, ultimately, forfeiting the part of the relationship in which mothers and daughters can talk and share the most important things with one another. Today's culture has convinced our daughters that we are irrelevant and wouldn't understand. We have accepted this as normal and lost a valuable tool of influence and the bedrock of our relationship with them. If we cannot talk to our girls, then what matter of influence and encouragement will we have with them?

The practice of how we use our words takes intentionality. Sometimes, our girls are plain tapped out. They are socially exhausted and need a break from the peppering questions. But learning the art of a mother-daughter relationship is a tender balance of leaning in and simply being available. It is our job to teach our girls how to use their words. Our daily habits reflect this, and our daughters learn what we model. Reclaim your place in the relationship with your daughter with your words and your actions. She hears your conversations, knows your sweet voice, your frustrated voice, and your not-so-happy voice. She has heard you use them all, in private and in public. Whether you know it or not, you are giving her language lessons every day. It's a lot to consider and can feel like such a heavy responsibility. Think of what is on the line, and add in heavy measures of grace, for yourself and from your daughters because some day they will be grown and mature, lavishly pouring out grace on all your mistakes. The time to work on your words is now.

Wisdom and Discretion

Every thought and action have a language of their own. If we were asked what we thought or felt about someone or something, we would have something to say. Our words have the power to edify, build up, or destroy. Learning a new language isn't easy but learning to control our tongues can be an even greater challenge. Biblical womanhood has a language of its own, and it begins with the root of our words. We aren't learning a new language; we are changing how we speak. God's Word clearly gives us examples of how our words should be chosen carefully. Our words come from the inside out. They are an overflow of what we put into our minds and where our focus lies. We may show more discretion in what we say and when we say it. Our words will become less hasty and more careful to show honor. Our speech will be seasoned with praise and not comfortable to gossip or slander.

While raising girls, it is easy to get caught up in the highs and lows of emotions, and the pressing needs we feel as moms. I am still learning to hold my tongue when I want to say something, react, or share my opinion. Discretion is a fruit of self-control and seeking wisdom—two areas I have been praying over for years in my own life, and for my daughters. Words harshly spoken are rarely forgotten. There is an appealing quality of beauty in a woman who uses her words wisely, who is not quick to answer, shows discernment in her reply, and most importantly, speaks words of wisdom. The habit of using pleasant words is a refreshing and sweet trait of a girl and a gift to those who spend time with her. She can be trusted with other's words. She will not react in rash defense, nor speak with foolish lips. A daughter who speaks highly of her parents and praises God with her lips has practiced discernment in her life and sought-after wisdom like gold.

There will be many moments in your daughter's life when she will be confronted with conflicts or situations where she may not have time to process a well thought out response or reply. She may not have the space to work through her emotions, or step away. How can a young girl learn to speak with wisdom and discernment? Are we expecting too much of our daughters at a young age to show wisdom in their words? The daily habits of seeking wisdom, practicing self-control, and thinking of others are great ways to begin.

Her daily habits might look like:

- Learning how to study God's Word for application; being prepared to give an answer for the situations she will face when we are not present to help guide her.
- Practice responding with self-control and choosing her words carefully.
- Making a list of what the Bible says are "good friends" and choosing friendships based on this.

How can we as mothers help our daughters use their words wisely? Start small and ask questions, like:

- "Did you think before you spoke?"
- "Would you want someone to speak to you in that tone of voice?"
- "Who were you thinking about when you said that?"
- "Was that really necessary to say?"
- "Can you say the same thing, but a little differently?"
- "How do you think that made the other person feel?"

I am reminded of a verse we learned on repeat in our home, from the time my children were little: "Gracious words are like a honeycomb, sweetness to the soul and health to the bones" (Proverbs 16:24).

Our tongue has the power to build up or destroy. I can testify that the very fiber of our mother-daughter relationships can hinge on our words. Let's lead by example in humility and by seeking wisdom from above. A mother can do her best, but it is Christ in her that leads her by His own example. When our daughters see the value of seeking wisdom, drawing near to the heart of her mother, and living out Christ's example with His power and Spirit, she will be equipped to be used by God.

Our words have power. How are we using them?

Gossip

Have you ever been at the receiving end of a slanderous word or gossip? It doesn't feel too great. Even more so, we feel overwhelming emotions when our daughters are the recipients of unkind or hurtful words. The added layer of self-control our mama hearts and mouths need in moments like these is what

I call abundant grace. It is hard to hear words hurled at others or stand in the thick of the surrounding whispers. I have seen gossip rip apart relationships, families, and even churches. This is how much words matter.

Gossip isn't considered a sin anymore. Instead, it has become a "you can trust me" vault of words that can cast a shadow on someone else's name. Women gossip over text messages, in the church pew, at the playground, and sometimes in front of their daughters.

Our tone, our timing, and our testimony are important when we speak about another person. Have we become immune to the habit of talking about others in the comfort of our home or with our friends? Do our daughters observe this in us on a regular basis and think this is normal and acceptable? Would our girls know that this isn't okay and why? Our habits define our actions, and our actions speak louder than words. We may be teaching our girls matters of principle, but if we aren't living those principles, what will our daughters be left with? Normalizing gossip is not okay. Let us be women whose words are seasoned with grace.

In Colossians, we are reminded that choosing our words takes work. It is important for us to remember we are accountable to the Lord for what we say and how we say it. "Let your speech always be gracious, seasoned with salt, so that you may know how you ought to answer each person" (Colossians 4:6).

Our Time

Every morning, over the last thirty-two years of parenting ten children, I gathered my children in the living room for a look into God's Word and to learn just who He is. As a homeschool family, we had the luxury of using our time like this when the rest of the world was already bustling about their day. With a lot of littles, it wasn't always easy, but I knew this was the one practice I wanted to be my forever habit—even a legacy.

With babies on my lap, toddlers restless with their sippy cups and snacks, the middles anxiously waiting to get their wiggles out, and teens, half asleep but present, we made it work. It wasn't perfect by any means. There were attitudes and whining babies, children hanging upside down off the couches, and schoolwork waiting for us to jump into. This daily habit not only drew us together, but it drew us to Christ. We studied His character, love, and mercy, and the stories of the Bible came to life in a way I am not sure would have if I had just assigned a Bible reading or devotional time for them to do in their own time. Making space in my mornings took great sacrifice of giving up "my time," and it is the one part of my life I will never regret.

My daughters learned so much in the time we had together as a family. We never made it about a check on our to-do list because then it would become something we "had to do," rather than what we would grow to "want to do." My girls learned the valuable life habit of giving God their first fruits with their time. We took our time in the Word and made it personal by choosing individual and family applications every day and week from what we read. I was never just the primary person to carry us through our morning times together. My girls practiced how to write their own devotionals, lead a Bible study, and engage with their younger siblings in reading and singing times together.

When our morning times were over, our daily lives were intertwined with the truths we were learning. We didn't just set our Bibles on a shelf and forget what we were learning. We found ourselves discussing how our lives reflect Jesus to others. Our faith became part of who we are and not just a daily checklist. Raising daughters who desire God begins with authenticity in your home and your own life. Our daughters don't want a perfectly curated faith. They need a mom who shows up in her weaknesses and imperfections, needing Jesus to give her hope and help. This is the transformation and reflection they see in you, through Christ.

Not only will time in the Word give our daughters faith-filled beginnings but will help them form the habits of guarding their tongues from negativity or gossip, learning who they are in Christ, serving others, finding rest in places of constant busyness—all will become pillars that stay with them for a lifetime.

Giving Our Time

When it comes to serving others, it is easy for us all to be motivated by being seen in our service. With social media shares and the opportunity to share everything we do, serving becomes less private and less personal. I have challenged our girls to learn to love and serve those in our home, before they try and step out and serve others. It is a lot harder to love and serve the people we live with every day than to show up for a few hours and give our time. Rosaria Butterfield says in her book, *The Gospel Comes with a House Key*, "Engaging in radically ordinary hospitality means we provide the time necessary to build strong relationships with people who think differently than we do as well as build strong relationships from within the family of God."[1]

My daughters served up turkey, mashed potatoes, and applesauce, elbow to elbow with my husband and me, at the local soup kitchen this year. Some of the girls were relegated to scrubbing pots and pans, and some chose to mingle with the locals who frequented this free, weekly meal. I told them before we committed to this area of service that there would be people different than those we usually spend our time with.

With our patterned aprons on, and serving spoons in hand, I watched the line begin to grow. There isn't really time for chitchat when you are serving food to those who have been waiting all day for this meal. Not to mention, I could see the girls work through their initial shock at the desperate state of health of some of our friends we were serving that evening—some barely able to walk or talk; many under the influence of drugs or alcohol and speaking unintelligible words; children wide-eyed at the feast before them, perhaps their first meal that day or week; and lonely people, desperate for a friend to talk to. My girls learned that evening that we weren't just serving up turkey and mashed potatoes. We were sharing hope. The girls quickly looked past infirmities and frailties to see others the way Jesus would see them. Our soup kitchen days led to food banks, nursing homes, hospital emergency rooms, ICU units, and homeless shelter ministries; we eventually took in refugees and homeless families. Our church ministries were and always will be important to us, but to be honest, having our daughters serve outside their comfort zones and see others in their most vulnerable places of life gave them a good dose of humility and a checked spirit of entitlement. Giving our time wasn't fancy or fabricated. It was a window into true hospitality and has helped prepare my girls for years of serving others in various capacities.

Mamas, expose your girls to people who are different, less fortunate, and in need of a walking, living gospel. Show them how to live out the character of Christ: by loving others. This habit grows humility in all of us—pointing us to praise and thanksgiving for what we have been given. Humility in a young woman radiates Christ to those around her. A humble spirit of giving and receiving allows our girls to be open to correction, not thinking more highly of themselves than they ought to.

If there is ever a character quality that shines Jesus in someone's life, it is humility partnered with gratefulness. Most everything we do flows from the heart. To whom or what we give our most attention and focus, is where our heart overflows into our lives. Give your daughters a daily point of reference for everything they do. The words they speak, how they make decisions, and the friends they choose, should all point back to Jesus: "Godliness with contentment is great gain" (1 Timothy 6:6).

Finding Rest

If there is an area that I didn't model well to my girls, it was rest. Maybe it is because with ten children I truly didn't have the time to rest, as we would think of rest in its most basic form. Sleeping was a rare luxury, let alone sitting down for more than thirty minutes at a time. Habits of rest are not necessarily defined by not being in motion. It has taken me years to understand what it means to find true rest.

I have had conversations with my older daughters as they watch me slow down, misjudging this as my age catching up with me. While there may be a tad of truth in this, the other side of the story is that I am now able to understand what rest can look like.

Naturally, I can't define rest for every season and for everyone, but finding it is the goal. With my three teen daughters left at home, I am currently trying my best to model what this looks like to them, hoping to avoid an unhealthy balance of serving and resting. One without the other leads to the bad habit of burnout and poor health. Looking for the moments to stop and listen to my family, or to lean in closer to someone's story are forms of rest. We are actually turning our attention away from our busy energy and allowing God to use us in the ministry of bringing hope and healing to others. Sitting down to listen to worship music, pulling over on the side of the road to pick a bouquet of flowers for my windowsill, planting flowers, or coffee with a friend, are all examples of rest. But true rest is found in Jesus, and usually when I am "doing" those things that involve serving others for His glory, I am filled with a peace that far exceeds a nap or reading a book. It is in the doing of good for others that we can bring rest to a weary world and to our anxious hearts.

Finding a rhythm of rest is important to teach your girls. If all they see every day is a woman running on empty, pulling her hair out, and complaining about how busy her family keeps her, then they will confuse serving others with stress. Show them intentional steps to making time in their schedule to delight in His creation. Help them create a schedule that balances serving and work. Remind them that God should never be drowned out by the noise and chaos of this world. He delights in our presence. It is there we find true rest.

Our Treasure

When I was first married, another woman in my church took me under her wing. I didn't realize it at the time, but she was in fact mentoring me. We spent time together as friends, but during that time, I was learning from her at every turn.

She taught me skills I use in my home today, things I would have never known if she had not taken the time to show me. And she taught me how to pray. When I knew prayer only as a checkbox and a few words to say that sounded right, she encouraged me to take my words to Jesus and to make my prayer a conversation, a plea, a repentance, and a time of praise and thanksgiving, reminding me that God was my Father and He wanted me to come to Him. She taught me the heart of hospitality, and the unselfish sacrifice it takes to serve others for the sake of the gospel and not for gain or glory. Her family adored her; her lips never spoke ill of other women. Drama didn't follow her, and when the drama came her way, she engaged biblically and with great wisdom and discernment. She didn't lay up storehouses of gain in clutter. She was a thrifty shopper, used her time wisely, and everything she put her hands on had an eternal purpose. She wasn't perfect, and I didn't expect her to be, but she treasured her family and Jesus, and everything else was an overflow.

Reflecting on those years, I remember how she modeled her faith in her daily life, teaching me by her actions. I remember her words being seasoned with grace, and her hours spent on eternal pursuits. In following Jesus with her whole heart, soul, and mind, she was able to create a legacy that reached beyond than her family.

I am going to be completely transparent and tell you that the word "legacy" was a concept that seemed out of reach and unattainable to me while I was in the early years of raising my children. No one ever explained what this meant, let alone how to create a legacy. Were there steps to achieve this lofty goal? Perhaps a formula I could follow or a book like this one that I could read, so that I could one day look back, knowing I had created a legacy? This woman had given me a real-life picture of what a legacy is and what it means. She showed me that her daily habits and choices were about intentionality and pursuing a relationship with Jesus. I wanted a legacy of faithfulness to pass on to my children too.

Our daughters observe our daily habits, what we do with our time, and just how much our words match our actions. Yet, one of the largest impacts we have on our daughters is the intentional investment we make in developing a sincere faith: spending time in the Word with our girls and helping them learn more of who Jesus is to them and why they can trust Him with their life. When our daughters see the reflection of Christ in our words, our time, and our actions, their identity becomes about what they see in the "mirror" of their mothers: Christ in us.

We're all a work in progress. With Christ's help, we will mature, change, and put former things away. Some things are harder to put off than others. This chapter is as much about us as it is about our daughters. Sure, they hear and see what we do, and eventually choose their own way, but it's the habits we live day in and day out that stick. It's the unconscious behavior that we grow to think is normal and not held to a litmus test. Good habits are fine; godly habits are what gives our girls the sparkle of the gospel that others can see and know "something is different about that girl." Something stands out and looks different: It is Jesus in her; Jesus, who can take the things we put off and help us put on the new.

Our habits are determined by our focus on our treasure. What will your daughter see in you?

A MOTHER'S REFLECTIONS

- What kind of words does my daughter hear me speak?
- How does she see me spending my time?

WHAT'S A GIRL MOM TO DO?

- Take one full day this week and pay attention to what your daughter talks about, who she talks to, and where she spends most of her time. Listen to her conversations, ask her questions about others, and ask her permission to look at her text messages. Take note of her pursuits and interests, look around her room and on her walls. Then take a day and give ear to your own words and what your conversations are centered around; consider where most of your time is spent.
- What an eye opener! When we pay attention to what we focus on, we can see who we will become. Every day is full of habits, determined by our focus. We are living the overflow of where the desires of our hearts lead us.

A MOTHER'S PRAYER

Lord, change is hard, and this chapter is a heavy weight of responsibility. Help me to discern the small areas I can identify in my own life that would be a good place to begin making changes. Help me be a good example with my time, my tongue, and where I am storing up treasures. Help me to keep my eyes on You. In Jesus' name, Amen.

8

Friends and Boyfriends

"IS SHE A GOOD FRIEND?"

"What do you mean a 'good friend?' She is my friend."

"Does she ask you how you are? Can you trust her with your words? Does she gossip about other people?"

"Mom, can I just have friends without you asking me all these questions? I just want to be friends."

"I'm glad you have so many friends. I think it's important for you to know you will have various kinds of friends as you grow up. You'll have friends, and then you'll have good friends. Not everyone knows how to be a good friend. If you want good friends, you'll need to be one first."

"Okay, Mom." (Sigh.)

This is how the friend conversation went with each of my pre-teen daughters. Sometimes it was received and sometimes it wasn't. Still, we avoided a lot of friendship drama in our household by making a "friend and good friend list." When our girls were little, everyone was their friend. They had play dates and no one thought about who was "cool" or "fun." They played, talked endlessly, baked together, went for hikes, and planned their weddings, travel, and dream jobs together. We all know that the core group of friends our little girls have now will dwindle and change over the years. This is harder for our girls than it is for us because we have experienced it and know it is coming. But this transition can be tricky for our daughters. They may take it personally and experience feelings of dejection, confusion, or loneliness. I've used this gap of time to have sincere and helpful conversations about friendship.

To avoid controlling or micromanaging our teenage daughters' lives, preemptive discussions like these are so beneficial before our girls come face to face with confusing or hurtful situations.

"I thought she was my friend. Why would she embarrass me in front of everyone?"

"Was she a good friend to you?"

"What do you mean, a good friend?"

"Remember the list we made that described the difference between a good friend and a friend?"

"Yes."

"What kind of friend is she to you?"

"Just a friend, I guess."

"A bad friend?"

"No, I guess, just not a good friend. I still cannot believe she did that to me."

"I'm sorry. I know this is disappointing. Let's look at that list again and see what happened."

"Thanks, Mom."

You will never really be done having these talks with your daughters. People change. Even good friends may come and go. But, above all, have the talks and keep current. If they cannot come to you and you don't have sound advice or even a word of comfort for them, then who will? Their friends? Moms, be the good and the godly friend. Learn to be a listener and not an "I told you so-er." Friendships can be hard for women. Eventually, we all figure it out, or at least hope we have. Guiding our daughters through the give and take of sharing their life with another person requires us to set our own feelings about the situation on a shelf for a while, so we can help them think through the relationship. Again, this is another example of handing over the baton of ownership to them.

When they are little, we interject and give helpful sharing and caring suggestions and pep talks; but when they begin choosing their friends and select groupies, we are on high alert to what is or could be. Be cautious to not meddle, but to delicately mentor. By this point we want our daughters to know we (prudently) trust them, yet we are still guiding them through life, as they learn to seek wisdom and use discretion. There isn't a guidebook for your daughter to find good and godly friends. Wouldn't that be an easy way out for us? No one knows your daughter like you do, and no one else has the bird's-eye view that you do on the people she is choosing to spend her time with.

Below, I've listed helpful guidelines I've used to navigate friendships through the years. As my girls had highs and lows in their friendship journey, I would ask the following questions and talk through the "real friend" list. Perhaps you will find this list helpful as well.

"Just" a Friend:

- Someone who is just a friend is friendly.
- Someone who is just a friend has shared interests.
- Someone who is just a friend can have a positive attitude.
- Someone who is just a friend is fun to be with.

Below are helpful questions our daughters can ask themselves. What might they add to this list?

A Good Friend:

- Am I a good friend who has others' best interests at heart?
- Am I a good friend who is loving? (1 Peter 4:8)
- Am I a good friend who is encouraging? (1 Thessalonians 5:8)
- Am I a good friend who is known for doing good for others? (Hebrews 10:24)
- Am I a good friend who forgives? (Colossians 3:13)
- Am I a good friend who is helpful and wants the best for others? (Ecclesiastes 4:10)
- Am I a good friend who doesn't speak evil against another? (James 4:11)
- Am I a good friend when times are hard? (Galatians 6:2)
- Am I a good friend who is trustworthy and loyal? (Proverbs 18:24)

The prompts below are suggested conversation starters. Our girls are smart cookies. You'll be pleasantly surprised with the ideas they come up with to add to this simple starter list. I recommend giving your daughter time to mull this list over for a few days and then revisit the conversation and review her own thoughts.

In the meantime, leave them with the following "How to Be a Good Friend" list. This will help them consider who and what they are looking for in a good and godly friend. Above all, enjoy the conversation. Their hearts are most likely in a tender place right now, and it's important to tread carefully with your suggestions. Betrayal or any form of a broken relationship is confusing and hard. I'll leave you with this good friend list, and you can take it from there.

"How to Be a Good Friend"[2]

- Good attracts good. I will be the type of friend I would like someone to be for me.
- I will take ownership when I am wrong.
- Not every friend is perfect, and neither am I.
- I will show dignity and loyalty. I will have my friend's back.
- I will learn how to lift my friends up, rather than focus on their weaknesses.
- I won't follow those who don't make good choices.
- I won't set up expectations my friends should not have to meet.
- I won't use manipulation to get my way.
- I won't let drama follow me.
- I will treat others the way I want to be treated.
- I will be the "go the extra mile" kind of friend.
- I will be trustworthy.
- I will be patient. No one is perfect.

And above all, teach your daughters that they can be friendly, while still not being good friends with everyone. We are not excused from living out the fruit of the Spirit in our everyday lives, showing kindness to everyone, releasing the expectation of deep and lasting friendship with all.

Remind your daughters of those fruits and qualities listed in Scripture:

"But the fruit of the Spirit is love, joy, peace, forbearance, kindness, goodness, faithfulness, gentleness, and self-control." (Galatians 5:22 NIV)

"And let us consider how we may spur one another on toward love and good deeds, not giving up meeting together, as some are in the habit of doing, but encouraging one another—and all the more as you see the Day approaching." (Hebrews 10:24–25 NIV)

We are reminded that the true meaning of friendship is sacrifice. In John 15:9–15, we read:

As the Father has loved me, so have I loved you. Abide in my love. If you keep my commandments, you will abide in my love, just as I have kept my Father's commandments and abide in his love. These things I have spoken to you, that my joy may be in you, and that your joy may be full. This is my commandment, that you love one another as I have loved you. Greater love has no one than this, that someone lay down his life for his friends. You are my friends if you do what I command you. No longer do I call you servants, for the servant does not know what his master is doing; but I have called you friends, for all that I have heard from my Father I have made known to you.

Take time to write these verses out for any relationship your daughters will have, now or in the future. Do I take the initiative in my friendships?

No list is going to help your daughters navigate every matter of the heart. That will be your job. Over the last three decades, I've spent countless hours with my girls sprawled out on my bed talking about life, friends, boys, and Jesus. As their mother, I have become "home." It doesn't matter where I am, they find me. They share their burdens, their tears, excitement, pain, worries, and plans with me. When they are quiet, I know something is brewing. Rather than prodding and pulling everything out when my alarm bells are going off, I have learned to let the matters of their heart simmer, allowing the Holy Spirit to do His work before I enter the picture. Watching them struggle and work through things on their own is hard. I can see it tearing them apart, keeping them awake, silencing their normal chatter. This is the sweet spot of surrender that moms of daughters learn over time. Give them room to go to God and then give them the opportunity to come to you. Don't chase their hearts down and demand they "spill the beans." After a period of waiting and praying, I'll gently lean in and ask, "Are you okay?" This breaks the dam, allowing the tears and thoughts to spill over. Sometimes, our daughters will surprise us and work through their problems in the "mulling over time."

If we give them the proper tools of communication, decision-making, and prayer, they can work through those matters of the heart. This is the goal! Right?! I like to think I go from living in a whirlpool of conversation and tears to being on standby. A mom's standby is a place of honor. Don't begrudge the day she doesn't come to you right away or doesn't "need you." That day is coming, and it is an answer to the prayers you've been faithfully praying for your dear and precious girl for years.

Boys, More than Friends

Can't our girls just stay little forever? The sweet friendships our daughters make with girls and boys alike is so innocent and perfect. The days of little to no drama slowly fade away. Those simpler days are replaced by times of hormones causing hyper-fixated thoughts about one person while the world continues spinning around them--everything is about one particular boy. This usually only lasts for a few days, because reminding our girls to eat, to stay focused on school, family, their friends, and keeping them engaged in everyday life is more important than a fleeting infatuation.

This is the perfect segue to talk about the friendships our girls will have with boys. Every or any relationship our daughters develop with a boy should always begin with friendship. In the process of working through the boy meets girl and what comes next, the friend list will expand from good friend to boyfriend. You will be grateful for this helpful tool in the future. Remember, for all the positive points to each list, we will also be able to help our daughters see the flip side to the coin. When emotions are running high and they are knee deep in sweet notes and flower petals, their mind will become a little muddied with loyalty and commitment. This is the nature of any relationship. The best advice I can give is to not try and control your children's relationships. Be available, give prayerful advice, and stay involved. Do not ignore red flags with the hope that things will get better. Give your daughter the confidence to make good decisions. Raising daughters who fall for a guy is different than raising boys who fall for a girl. The dynamics at home are different. The heart is deeply vested, so don't treat your daughter's affections the same way you would if they are choosing friend groups. Her heart is not an experiment, so don't treat this lightly.

Part of raising daughters is giving space for their dads to have an important place in their lives. Not all girls have this relationship with their fathers, but if they do, then help foster a relationship that gives honor to the place their dad can have in their lives. Dads are part of raising daughters too. In our circles, my husband is known for his "meet with the boy" meeting where he asks questions of each young guy who has an interest in our girls. He honors our daughters first, by asking them if they are interested in dating the gentleman before even considering a meeting with them. Those poor fellas; they must have nerves of steel. I am always impressed with the bravery they muster to meet with him. My husband is a softie, and everyone who knows him would tell you this, but there is a hype to meeting with any girl's dad, and this sifts out the serious from the fleeting "date for fun" crowd of guys that have lined up at our door. The meetings are casual in nature, and my husband tries to put the young fellas at ease right away. Of course, if he sees major red flags, the young man gets an extra vetting. The dad dates always end with a light-hearted tone, and everyone survives that first meeting.

I've seen the scene on repeat over the years. Our daughters are waiting for their dad to come home and share his thoughts and the outcome. They ask all the questions, and being the non-wordy kind of guy that he is, he doesn't usually remember too much unless asked specific questions. The air is thick with chatter and excitement, laughing at the jokes he made to those gentlemen to lighten the mood, and instant mortification and embarrassment by our girls. "Daaaaaaaddd! You didn't! Why did you say that? What did he say? Was he nervous? How did it end?" This usually goes on for what feels like forever. I am an observer in this unfolding scene before me, trusting that my husband asked the right questions and the boys had good answers, and that in the end, all would be well. It really is like an interview when you put it simply. But so much more. My husband shares his heart about our daughter, talks about faith and asks them to share their testimony, and gets to know more about them.

I asked my husband if I could share his list of topics and questions, and he was happy to share as well. By no means is this list exhaustive or the right fit for everyone, but this is a compilation of his discussions over the years. We hope you will find it helpful. If you're raising daughters without a dad, this list can be for you, or someone you trust to fill in the gaps to protect the hearts of your girls. That is the true purpose of the meeting times—to protect their hearts.

Questions Worth Asking

Below you will find important questions and conversation starters we have had with our daughters and the suitors interested in dating them. Don't shy away from the awkward questions from the beginning. Some questions may provoke ideas they have not yet considered. The conversations you have with your daughter will help prepare her for the questions she will need to ask herself when the time comes for her to begin dating.

Suggested Talking Points

- Why do you want to date my daughter?
- What is your relationship with the Lord like?
- Because pornography is so pervasive and accessible in our society, my husband asks, "Do you struggle with pornography, and if so, what are you doing about it/ seeking accountability?" (Struggling may or may not

be a disqualifier for you personally. Following up on accountability and next steps for them would be important.)

Next Steps in the Conversation

- Share a list with the young man of what you allow and don't allow. Your list will look different than mine. Here is an example of some areas we discuss: Avoid being alone together in a car or home, and discuss physical boundaries you would like the couple to follow.
- Convey to him that you take your role seriously to protect your daughter's heart and purity for whoever God has for them in the future.
- Tell him you expect him to protect her heart and her purity. Give examples of what this looks like.
- Explain that God created us with passions that are good but only in the context He's created them for; that kissing is too physiologically provocative and should be avoided until you are at a place in life with a time frame that allows you to "hold out" for marriage.

Dating Conversation with Our Daughters

There are girls who talk about boys/boyfriends at a young age. There are girls who make it all the way to college and don't have the time for "such nonsense." There's nothing wrong with little girls noticing boys.

The conversations we have with our little girls into their adult years will dictate their feelings, viewpoints, and healthy responses and actions toward the opposite sex. We seem to think we have time for "that conversation." If your little girls are talking about boys, it is time to have chats about their feelings and encourage them to apply the same friendship questions to relationships with boys they are interested in. We've always erred on the safe side of dating boys when they are mature, more independent, and closer to the age when they are making grown-up decisions and showing markers of maturity and thoughts to their future. Otherwise, we're inviting unnecessary drama into our daughters' (and our) lives when friendships with boys will do for now. Don't encourage a relationship your daughter isn't ready to handle on her own. Allow her the freedom to enjoy her friendships, work, and school, free from a season of expending her focus and energy to a relationship she isn't currently able to commit to. Let them be girls.

I walk at the local park quite regularly. In the time it takes me to walk four laps around the park, I have seen a lot of relationships. This park borders the local high school and seems to be the place where couples like to sneak away to be alone. The couples I have observed are young, younger than I remember having the kind of feelings they are feeling at such a young age. I want to stop in my tracks and ask those young girls if they are okay, if their moms know they are there with a boy. But I won't stop. Raising daughters who are confident in their skin with or without a boy's attention and affection takes intentional work.

While it is easy to read those words in a book, it can be much harder in real life. Because God made the beautiful design for man to be with woman, therefore, we all are naturally drawn to finding that person.

I've added several truths and thoughts we have taught our daughters from the time they are little until the day we give them away. Truths that pierce their heart where the stirrings of emotions will also reside when they meet "the guy."

Take these thoughts, and speak them over your little girls, reminding them who they are.

Dear Daughter, Truths for You

- You are a child of God, and He loves you more than your dad or I or any boy could.
- You are more than your body. Your mind and spirit are part of your beauty. Don't give that away to just anyone.
- Boys can be best friends. Enjoy those moments. Not everything has to be turned into dating.
- Dress for success and not for anyone else.
- Carry yourself with dignity and grace. This is a wardrobe of its own.
- Guard your tongue. Your words can tell people more about you than anything else you try to portray.
- Don't waste your time on relationship drama. If it comes to that, then let it go with dignity.
- See others the way Jesus sees them. This will transform how you treat others.
- You don't need to chase a boy. He will seek you out if he's the right one.
- Don't expect your friends or boyfriends to reciprocate the same choices you have made for your life. You may have to make hard decisions with people you thought you once knew.

- Let your words be seasoned with grace and honor the Lord. A friend or boyfriend who mocks your efforts is not worthy of your time.
- Don't change who you are. You are perfect just the way God made you.
- Your body is beautifully yours, and if you marry, then your body also beautifully belongs to your husband.
- No one can steal your joy.
- A boy that honors your body, soul, and mind, will become a man who will do the same. Don't settle for less.
- A boy who is intimidated by your mind or demeans you now is not your future. Choose wisely.
- Don't let the world rob your joy of friendships with the pressure to have or be more.
- Don't give others something bad to say about you. The world will always find something to say. It is how you handle it that reveals the truth.
- Honor God, above all else. You'll never regret this decision.

A MOTHER'S REFLECTIONS

- While you are preparing your heart for the day your daughter sets her eyes on a boy, consider the character qualities she will need to make wise decisions when that day comes. Your relationship with her now and the listening skills you are instilling in her will help keep her connected to you and seeking your advice as she navigates new relationships.

WHAT'S A GIRL MOM TO DO

- Have your daughter begin making four lists, each prompted by the questions below:

  What qualities make a good friend?

  Write down the differences between a good friend and a boyfriend.

  List the qualities you are looking for in a boyfriend.

  Record Bible verses that describe a good and godly man.

A MOTHER'S PRAYER

Father, this new season of friends and dating is daunting, and I desperately need Your wisdom. Help me to carefully guide my daughter without suffocating her own wisdom and independence at the same time. Give her good and godly friends, Lord. Protect her from those who may not have her best interest in mind and from choices that would lead to destruction. In Jesus' name, Amen.

9

Good Christian Girls

THERE IS PRESSURE FOR YOUNG girls to grow up and be a "good Christian girl." They feel the weight of appearing flawless, kind, or godly at all times. The confusion between legalism and genuine faith can weigh them down. Their faith-based choices can create isolation or judgment in the secular world. Many girls equate God's approval with their ability to perform well, creating a merit-based mindset. This pressure can lead to an unhealthy view of what it means and looks like to be good or godly.

I am witnessing an entire generation of young girls reeling from extreme moral confines or rules written in recent books for Christian girls. I have seen these girls' distaste for the church and Christianity, and an aversion to anything resembling moral standards. Sadly, this generation is rebelling against confusing messages, running, and floundering from the perfection imposed on them for the sake of an ideal outcome. The conflicting messages our girls must face each day in their circles of friends are overwhelming and downright disarming, to say the least. I've raised daughters in three different decades, and I have never felt the struggle of identity and what it means to be "a good Christian girl" as I do every single day with my last three daughters in this decade.

We are raising a confused generation of daughters. I don't blame them for their questions around conflicting mixed messages on purity, identity, modesty, femininity, and their roles in and outside the home and in the church. They are seeing a generation of women who are struggling with their identity after sifting through a hefty dose of purity culture, submission, and enforced meekness for their roles in the church and the home, and a mixed-up definition of what femininity and beauty looks like. Can we sit in this space for a few moments and consider exactly what it means to be a "good Christian girl"? This chapter is not written with a list of rules, but with threads of hope moms of daughters can hold on to and then carry forward for the sake of their daughters, their granddaughters, and future generations. Our daughters have had a poor reflection in Christian culture of what it means to be a good and godly girl, and my heart breaks for their confusion.

Sometimes, we need to get back to basics to build the future. This is the hope and foundation I've laid for my daughters and hold on to for the generations to come. With every difficult obstacle this generation may face to live their lives for Jesus, there are just as many possible and positive ways to raise a "good Christian girl" without a negative or impossible stigma attached. Here is the hope: Raising girls who love Jesus is possible. It is not our job to micromanage or control the outcome, but to live transparently and wholeheartedly for Jesus in the world and in our homes.

Once He has their hearts surrendered, He can do all things.

Pressure to Be Perfect

The sanctuary was silent as I watched the young teen walk to the front and stand there, all alone. Her hands rested on her small but growing belly, eyes locked onto the orange carpet while two men from the church board shared her sins publicly for all to hear. Her choices were obvious to anyone who could see her. The church leadership stood on one side of the room and she on the other. She never looked up until it was her time to speak. She was told she needed to share her sin publicly and repent. With everything in me, I wanted to scoop her up in my arms and shield her like a mother hen with her chicks. The hardest part of this story was knowing the hidden sins of others, walking boldly around the church foyer, while this young girl's choices were seen by all. She had made a mistake, and she walked out repentant, still alone. I watched this "good Christian girl" grow up, walk through this unplanned pregnancy, get married, raise her own family, and stay strong in the Lord. Her story is the same as those of many others, but to different degrees.

Christians should be above reproach, serve with a smile, be blameless and pure, date for marriage only, read the Word daily . . . and the list continues. The Christian culture has mixed up truth with opinions, which has led to pressure and confusion for our daughters. What we adopt as truth determines the values we impart to our children. When deciding values or standards in our home, we ask ourselves the following questions:

What is truth? Do our life choices reflect truth and love, or have we created a false sense of security with a man-made boundary?

Girls often feel an unspoken expectation to always be the "good girl" who doesn't mess up. Not only do they feel like they are living under a microscope of other believers, but of the world as well. Has our culture created an impossible image for our young girls to live up to? Perfection is misappropriated loyalty and the fear of making mistakes. When we make God's Word a rule book, void of compassion, our daughters wrestle with who they are in Christ versus who they are to be for everyone else. Girls today feel the weight of appearing flawless, worrying more about letting others down when they make mistakes or struggle. Oh, the weight young girls carry when we send the message that good works are equated to their worth, rather than understanding God's grace and unconditional love.

The beauty of living in Christ doesn't come from our attempts at perfection, but through redemption and sanctification in Christ. How can we help our daughters grow in grace and not be overwhelmed by the pressure to be more or better? It is their walk with the Lord that will shape their characters, not a list of dos and don'ts. We need to equip them to seek God's approval over the world's, teaching them how to use discernment as they navigate secular influences. We would be naïve to think that our daughters will not feel the pressure of cultural expectations, conforming to standards of beauty and success. We would be wise to remember the loneliness and isolation girls growing up in a Christian home may feel as they choose faith-based decisions that set them apart.

What a big job we have been given. Thankfully, it is not our job alone. God has given us wisdom through His Word to help us give our daughters a foundation that will hold when they doubt or lose their true focus. At the end of the chapter, I've included topics and verses to give us all a starting point as we raise our daughters to keep their eyes on Jesus, the author and finisher of their faith.

Identity Crisis

As I was lying in bed this morning, I was praying over one of my granddaughters. She had a birthday this weekend, and I was reflecting on how fast time goes. My mind ran through the other grandchildren and paused on the names and faces of my two oldest granddaughters. I reflected on their personalities, confidence, character, and ages. I thought about how much they are going to change in the next few years. I know the timeline like the back of my hand. As I sit here typing, looking at the pictures of my own daughters hanging on the wall in front of me, I can recall the big years of change. Sure, little changes are happening all the time, but there are significant years when our daughters will work through their identity. As much as we like to think we've given our girls everything they need to transition through those years without questions or struggles, we shouldn't ignore the signs when they come.

Don't be afraid of these years. When you know something is coming, you have more time to be prepared. Hear me when I share that when your daughters hit ages eleven, thirteen, and eighteen, big changes lead to big thoughts and emotions. The word "crisis" comes from a feeling of being threatened or shaken. Some girls struggle with their femininity, while others struggle with their purpose, appearance, worth, achievements, or relationships. If we are looking for the bottom line of where a "crisis in identity" comes from, it can be defined as anything that could change or we have unknowingly rooted our confidence in.

While it is important to remind our daughters of who they are in Christ, we often neglect to recognize the most important part is not found in who we are but in who God is. We live in a world that is constantly telling us to "find ourselves" or for teens (and adults) to "know who they are."

Writer Sara Barratt explains that "identity in Christ" begins with the gospel:

If we disregard the important truths that we're loved, chosen, redeemed, and forgiven, we have a truncated theology of identity. When our default responses to important questions of identity focus more on us than on God, we settle for answers that mimic the world's self-focused approach.

"Identity in Christ" cannot be separated from Christ and all that comes within the message of the gospel—God's holiness, mankind's rebellion, and Christ's sacrifice on the cross. If our teaching of identity glosses over these foundational truths, "identity in Christ" simply becomes a Christian catchphrase that leaves the hearers wondering how to find identity in God when all they've been told is more about themselves.[3]

The more we know God, the more secure our identity will be. How does knowing God affirm our daughter's beauty and purpose? How does she work through the challenges of her changing body and combat the shame imposed by doubt or insecurities? There is a danger of rooting our identity in our own attributes or circumstances. Anything we look to for assurance or happiness, other than Christ, leaves us on shaky ground.

That isn't to say that the outward person isn't part of God's design.

Of course, some of these physical and cultural traits, like our skin color and our family history, are beautiful pieces of God's loving and intentional design. We serve a Creator who loves diversity and a Savior who clothed himself in human flesh. It would be foolish and even unbiblical to claim that the God who formed our bodies and wrote our stories does not care about these parts of us. But that's just it: these things are only a part of our design. They are not who we are at our core.[4]

My now eighteen-year-old was asked to share a message with her youth group this year. The verses she was asked to develop her talk around centered on identity. After study and preparation, she had a solid take on what the Bible was saying, but she was unsure how she would be able to share her personal story with her peers. You see, she was a real-life ballerina from the time she was four years old. She danced her way through hours of practices, routines, and special performances. Her body and feet were like one, as she exchanged her soft pink ballet shoes for hard tipped pointe shoes. I remember the day she was fitted for her first pointe shoes. I watched from a distance, as her slender foot was measured and carefully fit with different shoes for her growing feet.

With the long pink laces, she hung those pointe shoes up for the last time at the beginning of her sophomore year of high school. She had become chronically ill and spent an entire year resting, giving up her beloved ballet. She couldn't leave the house, spend time with friends, or do anything strenuous. Without warning, her life changed overnight, and everything she excelled at, and most of her time growing up, was gone. She didn't see her ballet studio friends anymore. She couldn't express her creative and artistic gifts where she excelled, and she lost a connection to an incredibly special and important part of "who she was."

After weeks of studying and preparing for her talk, she came to me a little stumped on the direction her words were taking. She knew her theology of identity, but she was stuck on how she could relate this to the students.

I asked her, "What has been a big part of your life that you would say has defined you?"

With deep thought, she responded, "Ballet."

I asked her how she handled this huge loss in her life over the last two years. Because she had been bedridden, she and I were the only ones to shed tears over the magnitude and depth of those changes made in her life. She stood motionless, looking at me. I told her to go and get her ballet shoes. She returned with the tiniest worn pink ballet flats and her laced pointe shoes in each hand. I asked her if those worn-out soles were a waste of time. She shook her head. We discussed the life lessons she was able to take away from a hearty investment and spent time reflecting on how difficult it was for her to give up something she loved. While she was sick, one of the recurring conversations we had was about loss. She didn't feel tied to a purpose or people. Her time was wasting away, and she felt disconnected from what she once defined as part of who she was.

Our brave girl gave her talk to her youth group, sharing her story of time not wasted, but how we live in a world full of uncertainty. She encouraged her friends to find their worth and identity in the God whose Word never changes and is always the same. Helping our daughters find the balance of becoming a girl who does hard things, chases adventure, and does everything with excellence, is a careful lesson in where our affections truly lie.

Comparison Will Rob Their Confidence

I calculated how many total hours I have braided hair over the last three decades. With an average of braiding my daughters' hair only twice a week, for ten years, I've spent 1,820 hours braiding hair, so my girls could wake up with pretty curls and wavy locks. I've pulled back their braids for sports games and recitals and just because they wanted to "look pretty." The simplest efforts of love and care can take hours of investment. All our time cannot be summed up by what we do for our girls. Each of those 109,200 minutes I spent running my fingers through their hair were also precious hours of conversation. While brushing and braiding, we talked about their friends, their appearance, their confidence, and their fears.

A simple task of braiding hair became an opportunity for me to learn the hidden places of my daughters' hearts and minds. I listened to them express what they saw in the mirror and were feeling inside. With every braid and every conversation, we shared a journey of confidence, self-worth, identity, and inner beauty. For every word of truth I spoke to them, I was preaching to myself. As the years went by, it occurred to me that my girls trusted my braiding abilities, and we stayed focused on the mirror before us. They never really asked me to redo their hair. This was a lesson in life I wanted my girls to remember: They don't need to look to their left or to their right for approval or confidence. They could trust in a God who has their identity secure, and if they remained focused on Him, their beauty would stand out among the rest.

Comparison robs us from seeing the absolute delight God takes in His creation. Confidence and self-worth bring freedom. Your daughters will not spend hours trying to please others, allowing them to focus on the gifts and abilities God has given them. Creating spaces for vulnerable conversations fosters an open relationship where they can share their struggles, doubts, and insecurities.

How do we raise girls in a secular culture, where social media dictates a distorted body image and unhealthy life habits? Do we shelter our daughters from the world to protect their hearts and minds from comparison? How can we contend with the messages our daughters are hearing? I think we often resort to a shelter and a "hideaway" mode of protection. The mental health crisis is off the charts for the youth of today because the weight of comparison, paired with loneliness, is a dangerous mix.

Our daughters don't need a better wardrobe, cooler parents, or better bodies. They need moms who will stand in front of the mirror with them, talk and listen long, and model where true delight, strength, and beauty come from. Train them, teach them, and give them the tools and confidence to contend with the messages they will hear. It is our job to equip them to critically evaluate trends, friendships, and their choices through a biblical lens. Will they question their appearance? Yes. Should they steward their bodies and show wisdom in their choices? Of course. Do they need to compare themselves to someone or something else? No. When you are looking in the mirror with your daughters, ask yourself how they have seen you live in the shadow of comparison.

Think of your words and your life choices, especially the activities and social events you avoid or the friends you don't spend time with. What is holding you back? Where have you placed your worth? For years, I avoided large crowds, or any place where my words and my life would be the center of attention. I doubted my worth and was uncomfortable in my own skin. I had grown up without a healthy understanding of who God made me to be. When I stopped comparing myself to a self-made version of what I thought people were thinking of me, I began to speak to hundreds of women and confidently share what God had been teaching me about who He is and who He created me to be. My own daughters witnessed this transformation over the years, and it was the best testimony to true confidence rooted in His truth, far surpassing anything I could have taught them with my words only.

The "good Christian girl" doesn't need to live to please others. She doesn't have a different standard than the next good Christian girl sitting by her in youth group or school. Below are helpful ideas and Bible verses to give you a starting place for those intentional conversations with your daughters.

1. Schedule "heart check" conversations. Set aside time to discuss your daughter's thoughts and feelings.
2. Equip her with spiritual armor. Show and teach her the importance of Bible study, prayer, and community.
3. Celebrate her growth, and not just her success. Highlight her godly choices and character, even when outcomes may not be perfect.
4. Help your daughter understand healthy boundaries.
5. Live by example. In an age-appropriate way, be open and transparent about your own choices.
6. Pray with them. Pray for your daughter's heart, her friendships, and identity in Christ.
7. Teach her discernment to navigate secular influences.
8. Equip her to seek God's approval and not the world's.

"Do not be conformed to this world, but be transformed by the renewal of your mind, that by testing you may discern what is the will of God, what is good and acceptable and perfect." (Romans 12:2)

"But you are a chosen race, a royal priesthood, a holy nation, a people for his own possession, that you may proclaim the excellencies of him who called you out of darkness into his marvelous light." (1 Peter 2:9)

"For by grace you have been saved through faith. And this is not your own doing; it is the gift of God." (Ephesians 2:8)

"The fear of man lays a snare, but whoever trusts in the Lord is safe." (Proverbs 29:25)

"Charm is deceitful, and beauty is vain, but a woman who fears the Lord is to be praised." (Proverbs 31:30)

"So, whether you eat or drink, or whatever you do, do all to the glory of God." (1 Corinthians 10:31)

"But he said to me, 'My grace is sufficient for you, for my power is made perfect in weakness.' Therefore, I will boast all the more gladly of my weaknesses, so that the power of Christ may rest upon me." (2 Corinthians 12:9)

"For am I now seeking the approval of man, or of God? Or am I trying to please man? If I were still trying to please man, I would not be a servant of Christ." (Galatians 1:10)

A MOTHER'S REFLECTIONS

- Have I created an unspoken checklist for my daughter? Have I focused on outward appearances, or do we focus on the heart? Where does the motivation for growth and character in our home come from? Do I compare my daughter to other girls?

WHAT'S A GIRL MOM TO DO?

- I will focus on heart transformation, not just behavior.
- I will help her see that obedience comes from love, not fear.
- I will encourage her to walk with Christ in a way that is deeply personal, not just what is expected.
- I will remind her she is loved because she is His, not for being good.
- I will let her see my own need for Jesus, and not just my "Christian mom" side.

A MOTHER'S PRAYER

Help me to be a good example to my daughters, Lord, showing my daughter a real and honest faith that motivates her to love Jesus without performance. May my words remind her that You love her for who she is, and that her worth is not tied to perfection or outward performance. More than anything Lord, help me to lead her to You and remind her of Your love. In Jesus' name, Amen.

10

Preparing for the Future

EVERY DAY FOR THE LAST three decades of parenting, I have gone to bed completely and utterly exhausted. There have been occasional hot bath soaks, my bedroom door locked, and a smooth, quiet transition to my bed. But generally, one of two scenarios will take place. The entire household will be in my room while I am getting ready for bed, gathering as if they received a special invitation to a potluck where they each bring their highs and lows of the day, mixed with everyone's needs and schedules for the next day. Or there's the second scenario, which has become hysterically funny to me now that I am a little older. I am already in bed, my night routine is complete, I am cozy, and I'm just about to turn my bedside lamp off when they all march in, taking comfort on my bed, on the floor, and next to my face on my pillow. You get the drift. I am completely and desperately needed. (Loved.)

Don't get me wrong, I am thankful for every moment we have like this, even if this means I am exhausted when my light goes off at night. You would think that because we all spend the whole day together (we homeschool) that I would already know everything there is to talk about, and there is no stone unturned. I thought so, until I realized a few years into raising my children that those late-night moments are "bonus moments." The repeated conversations are not for opinion or planning. My children don't really want anything from me when they come in for those late-night chats. They just want to be with me and my husband: laughing, crying (that happens), and talking to us and one another about anything or everything. Those bonus moments have been my favorite by far as their mom. For years, I just wanted to sleep. *Please let me sleep*, I would beg silently. But now I realize the wonder of it all. This is where the magic of "being ourselves" happens.

When those deep conversations take place, all the teaching, planning, scheduling, and time constraints fade into the background. (Obviously, no one ever thought that Mom had a bedtime.) There we'd be, and still are to this day, one big, happy family getting to know one another when we can just be "us." No agenda, no constraints, and obviously no privacy. Because mom in her pajamas is not a big deal, and a handful of teenagers on her bed and on the floor, talking into the wee hours of the morning is the cool thing to do when you are that age. I think we have broken the record for "what is normal" in our home. We told our kids they would go into the world and be a shining light. We gave them the tools to discover their gifts, have good friends, stand up for what is right (and that doesn't always mean being the loudest person in the room), and set goals with eternity in mind. Now, those world changers make time for me, and I am in awe at the amazing people I see emerging from the tiny "plants" now grown—all from the comfort of my queen-sized bed, filled with teens who love to be with their parents. How cool is that?

Those bonus moments are a peek into their future. While they share their hearts, dreams, and plans, we get to know how to help them navigate the years to come. This is the exhausting yet daily work of guiding our children into their callings and the realization of their goals. How do we do this without crushing their spirit, trying to control the outcome, or taking away the hard parts of their story?

Goals and Gifts

When my daughter began to fall behind on every nature walk, caught up in the wonder of discovery, I "knew" she would become a photographer and a scientist. When her sister collected addresses, hung a large map on her bedroom wall, wrote letters to people across the world, and asked for a language video course for her Christmas gift, I "knew" she would work in communications and love to travel. Another daughter began making logos for fun, started two businesses by the age of thirteen, and turned her room into a prayer wall and Pinterest-worthy color palette. I "knew" she would someday become an entrepreneur. Some of my daughters, who are creatives, have turned their income and homes into an overflow of their gifts and creativity. Others, empathetic and compassionate, share comfort and a listening ear to those walking in suffering or experiencing trials.

When we recognize our daughters' gifts, the beautiful gift we receive as moms is a front-row seat to helping foster and grow those gifts and guiding them in setting goals that align with their gifts. I won't pretend this isn't exhausting. Like mining for gold, we can help our daughters discover and sift through the gifts God has given them. What may seem like simple interests or hobbies are clues to the areas you can help nurture. Pay attention to what sparks your daughter's attention, which interests draw her in, or where she spends her time. The clues are everywhere. What makes her light up, and what comes more easily for her? God doesn't hide His light under a bushel. When we teach our little girls the well-known song, and we teach them these lyrics, "This little light of mine, I'm going to let it shine, let it shine, let it shine," this is what those words mean. Moms, your daughters were made to shine. Once you see the light, keep it lit!

Every single time I am out with my daughters and introduce them to someone new, this is how the conversation goes:

Me: "This is my daughter, Maryahna."
Acquaintance: "Hi, Maryahna. It's nice to meet you . . ."
. . . "What are your plans after school?"
. . . "Where are you going to college?"

Sometimes, the questions are phrased differently. They have been asked which college they are going to, if they want to have a big family like their mother, or what's next. The culture today pushes a success-driven agenda, and young girls feel the pressure early on to know what they want to do or what their goals are. Some of my girls knew exactly what they wanted to do after they graduated high school, and others were still learning to navigate their new independence and balance their talents with their time. Those next steps will look unique for each daughter. Why not focus on preparing them to live successfully in the world, despite where they choose to go to school, which degree they are pursuing, or what measure of success we've deemed to be the path to their future?

I would rather raise daughters with a solid biblical worldview, strong and godly character, and a knowledge that whatever her future brings, she would be prepared. Success isn't defined by degrees or the highest paying jobs, although those can have great benefits. The perfect life isn't the proverbial white picket fence or the "perfect" sized family, although those can be blessings too. Daughters can feel pressure from the world and perhaps even parents or family members to check all the boxes. And although there isn't one right or wrong choice for each of our daughters uniquely, there are areas our daughters should have "checked off" before considering their future.

Rather than waiting until our girls hit junior high school to begin thinking ahead, begin when they are small. Keep an open mind as you consider the most formative and important areas you know they will need for the day when they take flight. Don't let it overwhelm you. You have time to help prepare them for the future. I've heard scare tactics about how time is fleeting and how quickly the years will go, but although this is true, there is a different way to think about the time you have with your daughter. You have years to be present and help her prepare. It is a gift for you to be right there with her and available as she practices her life skills in real time, rather than waiting until she leaves home.

Below is a list of some of the formative life skills and key areas on which your daughters should focus their time and energy as they prepare for their futures. Not all of our daughters will have an answer for those unexpected questions from well-intentioned people. But what they will have is an answer because their character will be shaped with grace and peace for what's ahead.

By no means is this a checklist for your daughters to earn God's or man's approval; rather it's a way to empower them to live out the calling God has on their life in freedom.

Suggested Life Skills to Practice for the Future

- Character and virtue that reflects Christ
- Financial responsibility and independence
- Time management skills
- Employment skill sets: diligence, good work ethic, accountability, flexibility, responsibility
- Mechanical skills: car maintenance, repair, and basic vehicle care and knowledge
- Technology skills: how to write a resume and fill out a job application online; other basic computer skills, such as filling out forms, saving documents, sending professional emails
- Good communication skills: keep current, tell the truth, be honest, ask questions, attack the problem and not the person
- Bible study skills and knowledge
- Ministry, discipleship, and evangelism; serving others
- Life skills in and outside the home: health care, meal prep, time management, laundry and housekeeping basics, home maintenance
- Social media etiquette and setting boundaries

The Path Forward

I would love to say the path forward is full of excitement, but I believe this is the most intensive work moms have set before them. Raising little girls seems like "fun and frills" compared to this next season of preparation. The hours of intentionality, sacrifice, prayers, follow-through, and celebration mixed with disappointment are like seeing the summit, but from the steepest part of the climb. You can do it, but you'll need an immeasurable amount of God's grace, laced with prayer, and a good friend to tell you to keep taking the steps. It will all be worth the investment, and through this book, I hope to be that friend to you when it is time.

You may still be pushing your little girls on the swing set, braiding their hair with pretty ribbons, and watching them make new friends. Wherever you are in your journey of raising girls to be women, this chapter will always be here for you to look back on for encouragement. Stick with me if you are making the climb and it feels too steep. The path forward can be taken in incremental steps. I've listed thoughts to help you stay focused on the journey ahead.

Fostering Your Daughter's Strengths

- Not everyone will see the gifts you see in your daughter. Be her biggest cheerleader.
- Find opportunities for her to try new things. Make it happen.
- Let her fail, try again, and learn from her mistakes. This will be hard, so stay strong.

- Pack your bags for the long haul. You will spend countless and endless hours driving and waiting.
- Be patient. Gifts take growing. You are the gardener.
- Find a way to pay for the special things. Some learning, training, or skills require a little extra. God always provides a way.
- Don't let her quit when she has made a commitment. Breaks are okay, and rest is necessary. But you are going to get those pom-poms out and cheer her on to the end.
- Celebrate her wins, small and large. Tell her how proud you are of her and invite others to do the same.
- Don't beat a dead horse. If she needs to move on, let her. Nothing is wasted. All the lessons and investment will reap a harvest down the road.

Wherever They Go

Your daughter has the fullest potential, and now is the time to give her the tools to be prepared for the future. As challenging as this may sound, it is a privilege to mine for the gold beneath the surface of all the noise. Everything we hope and pray for our daughters begins and is practiced in the home. The most rewarding moments are watching the gifts and talents you saw in your daughters when they were little come fully alive. Let's face it, motherhood is ministry, and whether your grown daughters work in or outside their homes, their lives will eventually be a ministry—even if they don't become mothers themselves. There are four areas I focused on while raising daughters to prepare them for this "ministry." Each category is taught and caught, meaning your daughters will learn from instruction and from living in your home.

Home and the Heart

A distant relative once shared their thoughts with me regarding my high expectations for my girls. Naturally, I was curious to hear more and to possibly gain insight on something I may have been missing while busy raising my family. I will be the first to raise my hand and say I missed many things, and I always appreciate when someone lovingly shares their thoughts about how I might do things differently. This conversation, though, didn't really cause me to pivot anything I was doing, but gave me an even broader sense of what is missing in the heart of many homes today.

When it all comes down to it, the word "expectations" is pretty accurate. This family member didn't understand why I assigned different jobs and taught various skills to my daughters when my girls could just be "enjoying their childhood." My daughters had a magical childhood. Growing up in a home nestled in the woods, the girls enjoyed forts, dolls, friends, stargazing, adventures, dress-up, and baking, to name a few—all the magical experiences we'd "expect" for a beautiful childhood. They certainly weren't robbed of fun and free time.

I tried discerning if this person was trying to say my daughters shouldn't have to do any chores, or if they thought my girls had to do too much. I took time to evaluate our home, our goals, and my expectations, and in the end, I came to this conclusion, and I still stand firm on it today: Girls grow up to make a home, with or without someone. They can learn with my help, or they can learn on their own later, floundering and wishing someone had taught them all the things they are trying to figure out, maybe while working, married, raising children, and suffocating under the pressure to learn it all now.

I think a better use of time and stewarding our role as mom and mentor is to teach and learn shoulder to shoulder and make a home with our daughters. It is shocking to hear from so many young women today that they were never taught how to manage their time, take care of a home, serve in a ministry, raise a family, steward their health, balance a budget, or make a meal plan. Should everyone know how to do one or all those things? I would be bold enough to say yes. This is what Proverbs 31 describes as a woman of valor.

We have become mixed up in our thinking that a home "maker" stays at home and does nothing. What I am describing is the ability or capability to manage our lives, and this doesn't mean "staying at home." It is our job to train our daughters to keep a home, to entertain, and to love the place called home; it's also to prepare them for the day they will need to "adult," carrying responsibility and care of others and their space, whether married, single, with children, or without.

Many women today have shared with me they were never prepared for this part of life. They just thought ahead to career and/or marriage and never learned how to be a mom or keep a home. Are we expecting too much by showing them that the heart of a home doesn't have to be drudgery and feelings of overwhelm but can be rewarding work for us and work that eventually allows our adult daughters to fit more into their schedule because they don't have to learn something new? Don't we want our adult daughters to live an abundant life? Preparing them with skills and a good foundation for their future is a gift worth investing in.

While our daughters pick up skills and life lessons learned in your home, the true impact you will have will be on their heart.

Hospitality

Our family has never *not* known the art and ministry of hospitality. We raised our children serving others, inside and outside of our home, from the time they were little. We hosted small and large events, celebrations, Bible studies, small groups, dinners, hayrides, festivals, and pancake breakfasts in our garage for Easter Sundays. We all serve together at food banks, homeless shelters, nursing homes; we clean or prepare meals, deliver care packages to hospitals, play games with residents in long-term care facilities, cook for church dinners, and more. Although serving others shouldn't be relegated to a long hospitality checklist, it is important to distinguish what we have done as a family and the heart behind a hospitable spirit.

We didn't open our home to always have a flurry of activity and a busy schedule. We didn't serve in our church and community for recognition or obligation. It was important to my husband and me for our children to grow up with a heart to serve others, and with the skills and the character to bend low in humility and deference. This is the heart of hospitality we wanted our daughters to leave home with. As they were growing up, we taught them to see and notice others with eyes like Jesus—for who they are in Christ and how we can serve them.

When my youngest three girls wanted to do a Bible study with their friends, they spent time researching study books and tools to pair with topics they wanted to focus on. In the end, they decided to take on the hefty project of writing their own Bible study. There is nothing better to prepare you for leading a Bible study than studying for weeks to be able to write the material. On top of it all, they offered to host their friends at our home. Ideas are always great in theory, until it is time to plan and execute the details. What began as a Bible study evolved into a weekly event with snacks, journaling, and a small hands-on project.

This Bible study moved my girls from helping and observing to planning and executing every little detail on their own. From menu plans to grocery lists, time management, cleaning the house, purchasing craft supplies, and hosting while tired, they learned how to serve others and enjoy the fruit of friendship and the sweet reward of gathering with others.

If you want to raise children who show hospitality, your job extends beyond the obvious expectations to model a servant's heart. You will need to teach your daughters how to plan, prepare, and live the "open heart, open door" quality. There is no greater opportunity for discipling your daughters than the practice of hospitality. I see discipling my daughters as a verb when they are little and a noun when they are older. The "doing" looks like teaching my girls how to cook or bake, so that one day they can serve others with this skill. I spend time teaching them how to read and study their Bible, so that one day, they will reap the fruit of knowledge and understanding. I encourage them to get out of their comfort zones in different ways as they are young because it is too easy to say no to serving if it isn't on our terms. It is human nature to avoid hard things. I allow them space to get creative and even messy. In an effort to simplify hospitality and make it more appealing to many, we often present it as something that just means "showing up." But I want my daughters to know that as much as that is true, doing things with excellence and creativity when you can is equally as important.

Their Bible study was not only a blessing to the other teen girls, but to them as well. While this was their first time independently taking on a larger scale form of hospitality, the small acts of service they show daily to others reveals a heart of discipleship, in both receiving and giving back.

Hospitality reveals our heart for others. We cannot always choose whom we help, host, or show God's love to. Hospitality isn't always easy, convenient, or comfortable. This is where we are discipling our daughters. If my daughters were the best cooks, bakers, craft makers, and hosts but had a spirit of resentment for the time they were giving or were serving out of obligation, I would not have taught them anything.

So, how do you help prepare your daughter for the future? Disciple her heart, for everything else will flow from this. Give her opportunities to serve alongside you, elbow to elbow. She will always be watching how you love in the moment and behind the scenes. Give her a chance to try new things. Encourage her to do hard things, and above else, remind her why you do what you do.

For every decision your daughter has before her as she launches from your home to find and make hers, she will recall your example, and lean into His Word with hope for her future. Below are a few verses my daughters and I memorized together. We often recall these and remind one another of these verses.

"Keep your heart with all vigilance, for from it flow the springs of life." (Proverbs 4:23)

"Beloved, let us love one another, for love is from God, and whoever loves has been born of God and knows God. Anyone who does not love does not know God, because God is love." (1 John 4:7–8)

"A new commandment I give to you, that you love one another: just as I have loved you, you also are to love one another." (John 13:34)

Discipleship

With the baby on my lap and two toddlers squirming anxiously for our morning devotional time to be over, I sat quietly and listened. I wasn't the one reading the Bible or teaching the lesson for the day. As my kids got older and morning time became a little "too childish" for them, I chose to give them opportunities to take part in leading their younger siblings and me once a month. Every morning I would teach them a character quality, a Bible story, a lesson, songs, and whatever creative element I would choose to add on that day. But once a month I turned everything over to them. I would give them two weeks in advance to prepare their short discipleship time for the family. They were free to make this time as fun, creative, or serious as they would like.

This time became one of my absolute highlights of raising kids in the Word. The more we did this, the more they prepared and became comfortable in their role as teachers, rather than listeners and presenters. Not only did the responsibility prompt them to get more creative, this pushed them to the Word themselves as they prepared. They would study the passages, write their own notes, and come up with amazing ways to teach the focused points they wanted to be sure their siblings caught.

My girls didn't realize that while they were being discipled, they were also learning the tenets of true discipleship. They started to see those moments as opportunities, rather than duties. Their interest in the Word wasn't prompted by checklists but finding answers for themselves. They brought the Word to the level of understanding of the listeners. They grew in patience, ditched perfection, and overcame apprehension of being in front of others. What began as something uncomfortable became a natural inclination to teach the Word and an example to others.

Discipleship is just as much about giving as it is receiving. It works both ways. I have been on the giving and receiving end of discipleship in different areas of my life. Our daughters will encounter many women in and out of the church who will call themselves mentors. It is so important to teach your daughters discernment and discretion. Giving your daughters a strong foundation of communication, theology, skills, and a heart tuned to wisdom will help her choose those who are sincere, good, and godly women. But, honestly, the Word of God is the best source of discipleship we all need. When we teach our daughters the value of knowing the Word, and even more importantly the God who loves us and His character, they have everything they need.

Communication

I am shocked to meet so many girls and young women who find it difficult to speak to adults or people they have never met. I am not referring to shyness or an introverted personality, in which easing into new and difficult conversations takes time but is possible. If there is a gaping hole in any area for which this generation is unprepared, I would put communication right at the top.

Maybe it helps to think about this in increments and helpful yet gentle nudges to prepare our girls for speaking up, speaking out, and speaking well. Sometimes, it isn't exactly what we say, but how we say it. When our girls are little, it is important to give them the confidence to speak when spoken to, to prepare them with an answer when asked, and to instill in them the courage to speak up when needed. I haven't met a girl yet, young or old, who doesn't love to talk, especially when she is comfortable and safe. I think this brings us full circle to their identity and how they see themselves in their own eyes.

Girls who feel insecure in their own skin will naturally have a difficult time communicating on most levels with others. They may second guess their thoughts, words and what others may be thinking. Girls who lack confidence in their purpose will doubt everything they do or say, hoping to blend into the background. Girls raised by mothers who are outspoken, brash, and always seeking to be heard above the crowd will avoid using her words altogether. What are we teaching and modeling to our daughters about communication?

Not only is it important for our daughters to grow in confidence and courage, but it is also equally important to communicate with honesty and a pure heart. Let's not teach them that the loudest voice in the room gets the most attention; although that might be true, the testimony of how they are seen and respected is altogether different. Not only is it important for our girls to learn how to communicate, but we must give them the tools to communicate well as they grow in wisdom and stature.

I've listed specific ideas that might be helpful for you to work on with your daughters as you prepare them for communicating with others.

- Teach them to articulate their thoughts when speaking to you, so they will be prepared to communicate effectively and clearly. Remind them to think before they speak, taking their time, staying focused on the facts.

- Help them formulate their thoughts into words while they are little. So often, their emotions are halted by fear or insecurity, and this in turn, can send mixed messages to others. Learning to express their feelings will also help them process them in current time and bring healing and clarity to them as well.
- Give them the tools to listen to a conversation and consider other viewpoints. Teach them to wait to speak, allowing others to finish their thoughts. Practice listening without a critical spirit. Teach your daughters to leave room in their opinions for change or growth. Often, we say more by listening than having the last word.
- Teach your daughters how to make an appeal. Rather than emotional outbursts, tantrums, shutting down, or downright disobedience, give them the words to engage in a disagreement with respectful questions and dialogue. "May I make an appeal?" would be a great place to begin while teaching this useful tool.
- Modeling when to speak and when not to speak will save your daughters from regretful moments.

Like anything we teach our daughters, remind them to focus their words on what is pleasing and acceptable to Christ:

"Let the words of my mouth and the meditation of my heart be acceptable in your sight, O Lord, my rock and my redeemer." (Psalm 19:14)

A MOTHER'S REFLECTIONS

- Have I considered my daughter's future through the lens of her purpose and God's will for her life? Or have I focused primarily on the next steps academically, professionally, and relationally, (e.g., her "married with children" status) that society generally dictates?

WHAT'S A GIRL MOM TO DO?

- Raise your daughters to be leaders who are patient, resilient, and persistent.
- Seek opportunities for them to practice living out their faith.
- Instill in them a biblical worldview. This shapes much of who they are and what they believe.
- Teach them empathy, compassion, discernment, and wisdom.
- Teach them God's Word. Study it. Discuss it. Have deep conversations.

A MOTHER'S PRAYER

Father, I am feeling overwhelmed at the thought of my little girls growing up to leave home, and yet, I know that day will come. I ask You for wisdom and direction as I guide them through the next years, preparing them for the future, whatever that may hold. In Jesus' name, Amen.

11

The Changing Roles of Mothers

MY BREATH CAUGHT IN MY throat as I looked past her shoulder to the reflection in the mirror before us. With her veil between my fingers, I delicately adjusted the cascade of lace down her back and shoulders. Time stood still, and this memory will be mine forever. Our eyes locked for an instant, and while marveling at the beautiful woman before me, I also saw my little girl in that mirror. I saw years of braiding her hair, rubbing her head when she was sick or afraid, and measuring her height on the wall. Mostly memorizing the reflection of Christ in her. I have seen the years of her gaze and focus fixed on Jesus. I have done my best to reflect Christ's love and character. I have looked at pictures from this special day, a few of which captured our special moment together. The photographs captured the emotion in my eyes, her gaze on me in the mirror, and a picture of love and release.

Looking back, I do not remember seeing myself in the mirror's reflection, but only my daughter and Christ. In that moment, my heart lurched into silence and awe, knowing that this has been a slow goodbye, and the goal was to see Christ in her, holding her, and going with her. I will always be her mother, but everything would be different now.

The Fun Mom

I have said this for years, and I won't deny it, but I have to work hard at being the "fun mom." With all of the roles I have had over the years, the serious side of me tends to rise to the surface more than anything else. I am still not sure how many people (including my daughters) know exactly what makes me laugh or how much fun I love to have. Motherhood is serious business, and somehow along the way, I have taken it a little too far. While raising my youngest three daughters, I have had more time to have fun and be a mom at the same time. Even when we try to be everything, something will take a back seat, and playfulness was the thing for me.

I love a good joke and a good laugh. I love to dance under a disco ball and leave my stress on the dance floor. I love funny movies, healthy sarcasm, and making fun of myself, because the Lord knows, I do some ridiculous things when I take myself too seriously.

As seasons come and go, your kids will be sure to point out areas where you may be missing the mark. Do they do this to hurt us? Most of the time, no. But listen carefully to what they say. One rainy day when my youngest three girls were little, we were stuck inside and looking for things to chase the long hours away. I told the girls to grab the games Candy Land and Chutes and Ladders. They excitedly ran to the game shelf and returned to me with anticipation and a few questions. “Mommy, how are we going to play these games if you don’t know how?”

There was a long pause and confusion on my part. “What do you mean I don’t know how to play the games?”

“Mommy, you’ve never played these games before.”

They were the last three of my ten children at home. I taught all of my kids how to play their childhood board games, how to ride a bike, tie their shoes, and the list goes on.

What could they possibly mean? And then it clicked. My littles didn’t remember me playing these games with them! They truly believed I didn’t play games. I had become so busy in all of my other roles as a mom, I had stopped being the fun mom.

I included this role as one to consider with all seriousness. It is so easy for us as moms to get caught up in being all of the things to everyone that we forget laughter and the fun-loving and lighthearted moments. Engage with your daughters on a level that takes you away from all other roles—where they see you sit on the floor to play board games, ride a bike, dance in the kitchen with a wooden spoon for a microphone, and above all else, having fun with them.

We will always have something to do, or say, or teach. Our girls will keep our schedules filled with activities and conversations until the wee hours of the night. Highlights my seven daughters recall are the moments when I let it all go and was just “Mom.” Make a list of all of the roles you show up to every day, and see if this encapsulates the mom you want to be. If your list weighs heavily on the side of parenting vs. enjoying life with your children, I’d encourage you to make a new column. Don’t let fears or time get in the way of fun and adventure. Take the time to laugh and live right along with your children. It's a role worth living for.

Loosen Your Grip

You may have the most "best friend" relationship with your daughter when she leaves home, and you may consider yourself to be the most easygoing mom in the history of mothers, but we all have a little or big grip on some aspects of control of our daughters' lives that we haven't quite recognized yet. I will be the first to break it to you: It is better to acknowledge that something will creep its way out and into your newfound relationship as a mother to a grown daughter before it takes you by surprise. You'll be prepared for the moment when your heart feels that first tinge of disappointment or feeling left out. Your response might take you by surprise, but this time to think ahead might afford you a grace period for yourself to autocorrect.

Your role as their mother is changing every day, but you never stop learning how to be a better girl mom. You may say goodbye to your little girls on a momentous day of release, but you are saying hello to a new part of the journey of raising daughters.

I will be the first to tell you how beautiful this next season will be, if you are willing to lean into a new role. The secret is this: You are in basic training every day while your daughters are still home. You are both training now for the future of your relationship and roles, as a mother to a daughter.

The very things that could potentially become a conflict or difficulty usually mean you have done something well. You've heard the idiom "too many cooks in the kitchen." While we are raising our girls to be efficient and comfortable with cooking and hospitality, we are crossing paths in the kitchen. We get in one another's way, have a different approach to a task, and over delegate to one another for plans and events. This challenge will be one of your first signs of success.

That dynamic will extend beyond the kitchen as your daughter gets older. She'll begin to "take charge" of other parts of your home, sharing her own style and opinions about your décor, your sense of fashion, how you use your time . . . and the list continues. This is the way it should be. We raise them to be creative but then are shocked when our living room has been rearranged or the spice jars are relabeled and in another cupboard. We teach them how to cook and feel a little put out when new meal plans are suggested or their kitchen needs conflict with our timing. We encourage them to find their style, and when we realize they love bright red lipstick and we've never worn a shade brighter than pale pink, you are left wondering whose daughter she is. We show them how to speak in public, be of good courage, not be afraid to try new things, and then they want to travel the country and study abroad. What happens when their successes feel threatening, step on our toes, or leave us feeling left out?

Let go, Mama. Loosen your grip on expectations before you are cut off without a thread to gently hold on to. I will be fully transparent and tell you it has taken me years to learn how to live in the process of change and how to live fully on the other side of the release. I want to encourage you to learn how to release control yet lovingly lean in and be there when and if needed. Oh, yes! You will learn how to be a new kind of mom, requiring a whole new set of skills with your character tested at every turn.

Leaving and Cleaving

There are a few words that might be part of your vocabulary as you watch your daughters take flight. These are words you might want to consider not using in this season, as a mother to daughters fully grown. Phrases such as: "I have the right to," or "I am your mother, " or "You should have . . ." Those words are not going to help you take on the new roles that include being available when and if needed, listening rather than sharing your opinion, and watching good and/or poor decisions come to life. I equate this season to the first two years of marriage or moving out or the scenario known as the inevitable empty nest pains.

Give yourself two years to learn your new roles, when to speak, when to insert yourself, when to be present, and when to step back. Ironically, our daughters are also experiencing a "honeymoon phase" as well, and have their own adjustments to make.

Try to be sensitive to the fact that as hard as the ever-changing roles and expectations are for you, your daughter is experiencing her own kind of homesickness. Oh, it may not look like it from the outside. She may be living her best life or hopelessly in love with the man of her dreams, but what you're not seeing is her redirection of thoughts, her processing, inclinations, needs, and her balancing of her time and affection. Her heart is also feeling the tug, and she is missing her mom, but she is learning to live "without" you.

We have four kids still at home (three teen girls and an adult son) and six who have moved onto new lives, which means we have experienced the leave and cleave process quite a few times, and it is surely something to be learned. Especially as a mother. From holding our tongue, learning our place, watching with admiration, showing unconditional love, affirming choices and giving wisdom when needed—I call this "the delicate balance." Mothers become a whole new person in this process, one that tells us who we really are and shines a light on areas we can work on as well.

I've outlined helpful reminders of who you are and what never changes. I have also added optional phrases to replace our natural inclination to be "mom first." Of course, lip service goes only as far as your words, so reorienting our hearts is just as important.

Who You Are

You will always be her mom. You've always been her cheerleader, front and center. You've cheered her on, celebrating her milestones, and you have always been her biggest supporter. Your role as cheerleader will now be from a distance. Your support is still vital, but done from the sidelines—sometimes silent, always prayerful, and less hands-on.

You will always be her safe place. You've always been the counselor and consultant, answering questions and guiding her through decisions. But, now learning to hold back when you want to fix a problem is necessary. Wait until you are asked and share wisdom with humility. Shift from managing her needs to covering her in prayer.

You will always be her prayer warrior. You will never stop praying for your daughters, but now you are reminded that, more than ever, you are not in control. If there is ever a season of surrendering your daughter and her life to the Lord, it is when she leaves home. Your prayers are more powerful than your presence.

You will always be home—a safe place she can return to whenever she needs to. This will never change. You will learn to cherish the new moments, rather than expecting her constant presence to define what home is to you.

You will always be a mentor. She is always watching, even from afar. The reflection of Christ in your life doesn't end when she leaves home. Your relationship with the Lord will deepen as your time allows more space in His presence. Don't ever underestimate the value of living on mission for Christ. You are always mentoring someone.

Who You Are Not

You are not in control of your daughter's decisions or responsible for her mistakes. Unless you've been invited into a space where she is seeking your wisdom or advice, your role is to listen, pray, and pray some more. Don't worry, she will reach out and bring you into her life. Wait patiently, expectantly, prayerfully, and humbly.

You are not her scheduler or time police. In other words, if you ever used guilt as a motivator, you are not that mother now. Instead of demanding time, work hard to foster a relationship they want to return to, extending love, grace, and understanding.

You are not the rival. She is not in competition with you. You are not in competition with her spouse, friends, or in-laws for influence, time, or importance. Just because your daughter's world is expanding, doesn't mean you are losing her. She is not trying to outshine you. She is not trying to overlook you. She is living the most busy, amazing, and big life right now, and rather than vying for her attention, be the cheerleader, the prayer warrior, and watch her life unfold and bloom.

As far as her earthly relationships go, you are not the main character in her story now, and it is not your role to always be lurking in the corners of her life, intruding in her marriage, her career, and her parenting, offering unsolicited advice. Step back and let her establish routines and make strong and informed decisions on her own.

Release control and step into your new roles of motherhood and the identity God has always given you: daughter. You are His chosen daughter, beloved.

Below are phrases for you to practice as you embrace every new season of leaving and cleaving.

Rephrase Your Words: A Leave and Cleave Vocabulary

Don't say: "You never call me anymore."

Rather, try this: "I love hearing from you. Let me know when you might want to talk."

Don't say: "I guess you're too busy."

Rather, try this: "I know life is full for you right now, but I am thinking of you and always here when you need anything."

Don't say: "I miss the way things used to be."

Rather, try this: "I love our memories and look forward to making new ones together."

Don't say: "That isn't how we do things."

Rather, try this: "I enjoy hearing your new ideas."

Don't say: "You need to be here for the holidays."

Rather, try this: "We'd love to have you, but understand when things don't work out. We can share your time."

Don't say: "I feel so left out of your life."

Rather, try this: "Let's work hard to stay connected in ways that work for both of us. Even if it looks different than before."

Don't say: "I gave up so much for you. The least you could do is give me your time."

Rather, try this: "I am so proud of the woman you've become."

Daughters-in-Love

I couldn't wait to write this part of my book. God has given me the absolute best daughters-in-love. I call them this corny, yet endearing name. You've been reading little snippets here and there, where I refer to them this way. Don't worry; I asked, and they approved. God gave me eyes to see them with the most unique perspective. I see the way they were mothered. I see what kind of daughters they are. I see them as the gift and chosen brides for my sons. What an absolute blessing to be given extra daughters. I've thanked their mothers for sharing them with me. God knew what He was doing when He chose these beloved women as helpmeets for my sons. They can see the vision and love I have for my boys, like no one can.

I not only gained new daughters, but I also passed the baton of my love and care for my sons to my new daughters-in-love. What a release that is! This requires trust, hope, and did I say trust? But watching them become part of our family (which is no small feat) and embracing all the different voices, opinions, and personalities in a family with seven daughters is one big task and calling for them. They have been champions! Has it been easy? It has been a journey we all took together, and if I learned anything through this process of learning and loving new daughters, it would be this: They are someone's daughter, loved and cared for, and God has given (entrusted) me to partner with Him in reflecting who He is to them.

When my firstborn son was newly married, I worked hard to live out my own advice and give the new couple the space to become one, not living in the shadows. I vividly remember one daughter-in-love inviting me to lunch. Just she and I, out for lunch together. I was a little nervous. *Did she want me to give them more space? Was I being too intrusive with my offers to help? Did I say something wrong?* Can you tell I was trying a little too hard to be the best mother-in-law I could be? This is a good place for me to pause and encourage you to take a deep breath, remembering we are all a work in progress. You don't need to get it all right, or even a little right at once. Grace will be your biggest friend in your mother and daughter-in-law relationships. Give and take; talk and listen. You can grow to become good friends. Your relationship can grow if you both stay engaged in one another's lives.

Our lunch was proof of this common foundation we all can have in Christ's love. We ordered our food, and while we waited, we talked about life, her new job potential, going back to school, and marriage. I loved every minute of our time together. While she was talking, I remember thinking how different she is, so talented and bright, and her words were carefully chosen and paced slower than the fast-talking daughters I had raised. I was learning what she loved, her interests, her goals. More than any other moment, that lunch gave me the most clarity for why God chose her to be my son's wife.

I had just taken the last bite of my sandwich when her next words broke through my thoughts.

"I wanted to take you to lunch to ask you something." She unraveled thoughts that had been building up, and she said she just needed to talk to me about it. She had friends "jokingly" ask her if she planned to have a "million children," like her mother-in-law. She said when she married my son that people assumed she would also have a big family. She had been feeling pressure from other people to be "like me," and she bravely and confidently wanted to convey to me that the pressure had become too much. She was clear that I had never imposed those thoughts or expectations onto her. This was just an assumption others had when she married into our family.

This was eye-opening for me as a new mother-in-law. The idea would never have crossed my mind. I was so thankful she took me to lunch to share this unspoken pressure of weighing on her heart. We had a great conversation, me assuring her I would champion her choices and would never expect someone else to live this unique life God called me to. This lunch was formative for me and for our relationship. We forged a trust and learned that we could talk frankly and openly with the other person. God gave me a gift of my daughters-in-love.

Daughters-in-love aren't your rivals. They are learning your family dynamics and gauging how to communicate with you and embrace you, while loving your son. Give her grace. Stay out of her business, and encourage her in the hard things. Champion her, like you do your daughters. Include her in all the special things, but give her space. A daughter-in-love is a grown woman, despite the difference in age between you. Show her respect, celebrate her strengths, and show compassion when she is struggling. We are all a work in progress.

Capture and Release

My daughter allowed me the honor to care for her while she was extremely ill this year. After laying down her little guy for a nap and setting her precious daughter up to color quietly on the couch, I turned my attention to the sink. Lunch cleanup was calling me. As I stood at her sink, I gazed out the window at the swing set, which had just held her children's laughter and growing bodies. As my attention was drawn back to the sink, my gaze rested on a new Polaroid among the others taped to the window frame. I remember when my daughter took the first Polaroid of her little girl and taped it there. Now, there were neat rows of her two babies, growing up in each photo. From their first bath and snuggles with their mama to their current age. I dried my wet hands and wrapped each arm across my body, embracing my own body and remembering my babies, from womb to raising their own children. These snapshots of her children's lives over a few short years are placed where she can reflect and remember but also consider the years to come.

Mothers never forget every little snapshot taken and stored in her heart. Like a million Polaroids taken and taped where we will never forget, each and every one is held in our memory bank. For every snapshot you've captured of your daughters' lives, they will forever be held in your heart and mind. When it is time to release each girl and embrace every new role, you will forever have those memories. We are never really saying goodbye to our girls, we are carrying our love for them with us into a new season. When I watch my daughters with their own children or see them walk confidently into their careers or new ventures, I am in awe of the story I have witnessed unfolding before me.

Moms, you have been given the very best, front-row seat to a beautiful love story. Our Creator God, who gave you your beautiful daughters, loves you so much. He wants you to bear witness to what He is doing and has done. Don't lose sight of the story being written just because you have a different seat now. You are the only one who holds those snapshots near and dear, and right now is the time to give praise to the Lord for all He has done in both of your lives.

As soon as we take our eyes off the past and present with fear for the future, we lose valuable time. We lose sight of His unfolding story for our daughter's life. We miss more snapshots of grace and beauty. He has prepared you for this moment. It is you, dear daughter, God wants you to see. He has done a good and beautiful work in YOU.

Do you see it?

"Remember not the former things, nor consider the things of old. Behold, I am doing a new thing; now it springs forth, do you not perceive it? I will make a way in the wilderness and rivers in the desert." (Isaiah 43:18–19)

A MOTHER'S REFLECTIONS

- How am I preparing my heart for the slow release of my daughter into the next season?

WHAT'S A GIRL MOM TO DO?

- As you recall snapshots of your daughter's life, attach a verse to each one, praying for the Lord to give her wisdom and direction in all her steps.

- Begin praying for your future daughters-in-love.
- Ask the Lord for strength and wisdom as you begin to guide your daughter toward her next steps.

A MOTHER'S PRAYER

Father, it is easy to make change all about us. Help me to refocus my energy and emotions to the rest of the Your story. I need your wisdom and peace when it is hard to remember You are in control. Protect and care for my girl, as I release my grip, little by little. Thank you for holding me—Your daughter—close in those moments. In Jesus' name, Amen.

12

Nothing Is Wasted

I DO NOT HAVE A perfect relationship with any of my daughters, but I will never give up on the hope for our future. I will never completely understand them, and I already know that I frustrate them to no end some days. They watched me grieve over the loss of my own relationship with my mother and stood by when I truly didn't think I would make it through. My daughters are champions, daughters full of grace and forgiveness. They are good listeners and even better talkers. Sometimes they speak to me as if I have a shield of armor over my heart, forgetting that I hurt too. Often, I slip too fast into friend mode voicing needs and wanting their time, forgetting they have lives of their own. We slip up, mess up, fess up, and grow forward together.

Some of us were raised by a mom who needed to be at the center of every story. She never held the mirror for us to see ourselves as His daughter, or loved lavishly, unconditionally, and completely. Some never had a cheerleader, a champion, or a mother who could see beyond herself to say, "I love you no matter what. Go and live your beautiful life. See what God is doing!" She made everything we did about her. She was the queen in front of the mirror, asking every day, "Mirror, mirror on the wall, who is the fairest of them all?"

I never could see the mirror as whole until I had my own daughters. Over the last thirty years, God has refined me in so many areas of my life. He has softened edges of anger. He has touched deep places of insecurity and healed me with His strength and faithfulness. He has replaced my fear and striving for the best relationship with my giving the best I can and letting Him have the rest. God has blessed me abundantly with seven daughters, replacing my pain with joy. He has shown me what it is to honor others and to let them shine. God graciously and mercifully rescued me from abandonment and restored to me the joy of my salvation. I can rejoice in the knowledge that my daughters walk in truth. Was this journey easy? Definitely not. Did I experience a transformation in my heart and especially my mind? Yes, a resounding yes. When I look in the mirror, I am whole, redeemed, and nothing is wasted.

Not all mother-daughter relationships are held together by strands of forgiveness, love, mercy, and grace. Somewhere the cord has been broken and has left a gaping wound for someone reading this book today. I write these words for you because you need to know it is okay to grieve what you have lost. We cannot pretend there isn't a hole in the heart of a daughter who lost her mother or hasn't had her mother's love in her life. You are not alone. You are beloved. Pause here for a moment and speak these words over yourself:

"I am His beloved. I am loved, no matter what."

Your relationship with your daughter doesn't need to be broken into a million pieces of insecurity and doubt. God has a special plan for you both, even when it is hard to see.

Now it is time for you to celebrate all God has done in your life! Look at your daughter with new eyes. Train your vision to see what God has done and is doing in her life. Let her choices or mistakes lead you to prayer. Cheer her on as she faces her future. Tell her how proud you are of her, as she chooses Jesus over everything. Give her the grace she has given you. You can change the course of your generation, breaking chains of brokenness. As you seek to become more like Jesus, she is living her own journey of growth and transformation. You are both fully known and fully loved.

As your daughter launches into her new life, you will face new feelings. You are still whole and deeply loved apart from your role as mother that you poured your heart and soul into for so many years. Your identity was never solely rooted in motherhood, but as a daughter of God. He still has work for you to do. Your calling didn't end when she grew up. All the seeds you have planted are still taking root and will continue to grow. Even when her path looks different from what you thought it would, God is faithful. When your house feels too quiet and the days feel long, remember you are not alone. Maybe enjoy a little of the peace and quiet? Your home will feel different, your schedule will feel empty, and your identity may feel a little mixed up, but this is a time for renewal. Your calling isn't over, and God isn't done using you.

Scripture assures us: "And I am sure of this, that he who began a good work in you will bring it to completion at the day of Jesus Christ" (Philippians 1:6).

Growing Pains and God's Love

My daughters have faced decisions and hardships that I could not have predicted when they were little. No matter how many good influences, Bible verses, godly character, or unconditional love they were showered with, the troubles have rolled in. We live in a broken world, and it would be remiss of me to think my girls would be exempt from the effects of sin and humanity on their lives. These moments are the litmus test to our own character. How we react, choose to act, and be present for our daughters will reveal much more of who we are than any other moments. I've heard mothers call themselves "Mama Bear," and others say, "They'll figure it out; we all do."

If my heart carried all of the pain and hardship my daughters have faced or will endure, it would surely break. As in childbirth, we feel their growing pains, as if it was our own to bear. Whether we witness our girls experience natural consequences of poor choices, injustice, physical stress, or broken relationships, it is also our natural inclination to want to take it all away for them. As much as we want to bear their burdens, we cannot. We feel this in our bones, in the deep recesses of our hearts. I believe this is one of the truest tests for moms: to trust their daughters' lives with the Lord. He is carrying them, holding them, and providing for them, and our muddled efforts to comfort or carry this burden with or for them is our way of loving them through. We can show up, help, and pray for them in whatever they may be going through, but in the end, we cannot lift it. Oh, how we wish we could. Watching our girls live out their struggles can be anguish, to the point that our protector and fixer role may rise to the surface. Oh, friend, this is so hard. Knowing when to be Mom and when to be the friend who guides and supports requires discernment on the hardest of days.

You will have conflicts and disagreements with your daughter. I would be surprised to meet a mother and daughter who agreed on everything and never had a miscommunication or disagreement. Those moments do not define your relationship. They may expose character issues or a root issue that needs to be exposed and worked through. This book isn't a guide to the most perfect mother-daughter relationship. You should not be hurt or surprised when the strong, confident, and independent daughter you raised has decided she believes something different than you. By the time my girls were nine years old, I could pretty much predict what we would disagree on in the future, where we might have conflicts, and what to expect in the coming years.

You can't fix everything, but you can own your part. Remember, just because you want to work through something or support your daughter through her challenging times, doesn't mean she wants the same outcome as you. Pay attention to her responses and her heart posture and determine your next move. Support, restoration, and conflict resolution can be taught, but you cannot force someone to believe you love them and want the best for them. They have to believe this.

When your daughters have been wronged, we would do anything to fix things for them. When we find ourselves in a situation where we cannot be the fixers, it is important to let Jesus take your burdens. You are not meant to carry everything for everyone. With humility, prayer, and forgiveness, let Him take this from you. God will fight on your daughter's behalf. He will make all things right. Nothing is wasted, so don't give up.

I've watched a few of my daughters face significant health crises, disappointments, and critical decisions that felt as if we were all going under. From serious accidents, physical and emotional trauma, and a significant loss, such trials made it hard for me to breathe many nights. As I lay down to sleep, I would replay over and over in my mind all of the things I couldn't do to fix or help or take away. I felt helpless yet didn't want to suffocate them with my worry or concern. That would be the last thing they needed. This was their story, and "all I could do was pray."

Here are some practical ways we can help our daughters navigate hard things and know they are deeply loved through trying times, when the only real and present love they are able to see in front of them is you.

- Be the listener.
- Validate the reality of their experiences.
- Be a safe space. You don't always need an answer or solution.
- Show up in their hard moments.
- Focus on the problem and not the person.
- Encourage them to find peace or resolution and not avoidance.
- Reflect on the things you can see as helpful solutions, rather than pointing out the mistakes.
- Remind them that conflict is inevitable, but what is important is how you handle it.
- Point them back to Jesus.
- Pray for their needs specifically.
- Tell them you will always love them, no matter what.

From the moment of little pink onesies to the change in home, career, marriage and/or children, our daughters are gifts to us. As complicated as it is to figure it all out some days, don't give up pursuing one of the best friends you could have in this world. When your daughters are little, you never want them to grow up. The love they show through their snuggles and their hands in yours will someday be expressed through a card in the mail, a hug when you get to her house, or a shopping trip filled with bargains.

Someday, she will be there for you, caring and listening when your heart can bear no more. She will laugh with you, have tea with you, pray for you, and be there to just be there. And if she isn't, you can rest patiently in this: You will love her no matter what.

A MOTHER'S REFLECTIONS

Dear Daughter,

I was the first one to hold you, to look into your eyes, and to feel your breath on my face. I taught you most of your firsts and many of your lasts. I kept you alive when I thought it might kill me some days. When your blankie went missing, I made you a new one. When you needed a bandage, we colored a smiley on your arm. Your fear of the dark or your need for a quiet space was important to me. Even when I sent you out to take care of the chickens at night, I would stand at the door or send you with a flashlight.

Letting you grow up and do the hard things was hard for me. I would have taken all of the hard stuff away if I could have. I worried over the little and big things. I did my best to protect your heart from the world, from bad boys, and from the influences seeking to destroy a young woman. I held you when you were sick and burning up with a fever. I taught you to write your name in capital letters and then lowercase, first and last. When you were nervous over auditions or recitals, I wanted to let you stay home. I stood in the back, pacing, praying, and ready for whatever would happen. I sat for countless hours during lessons, knowing that someday you would use your gifts for God's glory, even if I was the mean one making you practice and asking you to try your best.

Your birthday came around every year as birthdays do, and I could say it was "left up to me" to make it special because who else would; but it was an honor, and while everyone was singing your birthday song, I was carrying the cake and watching another year pass with the blowing out of your candles. Your feet grew like weeds, and every time we tried on new shoes, me bending over to be sure they fit with wiggle room for the growth to come, I would whisper under my breath, "Lord, how can this be? Please slow this down."

When your friends abandoned you, and boys broke your heart, I brought the tissues and the chocolate, and we talked about how horrible other people are until we laughed and cried our hearts out. We all felt better afterwards. When you needed braces, or glasses, or surgeries, or emergency visits, I took you and asked God to get us through. When you wore the same outfit for days, and I made you take it off to be washed, you thought I was trying to upset you. When your dress was too low in the front, and I asked you to change or put on a sweater, you told me I was ruining your life. From late basketball games to broken bones, I was there. When you were in the emergency room and the doctor wouldn't let me see you, I wouldn't take no for an answer because nothing can stop my mother's love.

You wanted bangs, and I told you I didn't think it was a good idea. You got them anyway and still blame me to this day for "letting" you get bangs. You got stomach aches from spicy foods, and I told you to take better care of your body, but down went the chili pepper chips, and you stayed up all night sick. I loved you imperfectly.

I hope you can forgive me for losing my focus, in the moments I began to grow weary in my journey of raising daughters. I have always wanted the best for you. My love for you isn't a list of what I've done. It is my hope that you read between the lines to see my heart for you. You may never really know how much until you someday read this letter, and when you do, remember, it was all for you.

WHAT'S A GIRL MOM TO DO?

- Keep reminding yourself that your daughter's journey is just beginning. She will learn how to communicate clearly and biblically and will walk through hard times. Give yourself both grace and care.
- I will point my girls back to Jesus, the author and finisher of my faith. May she see His work in my life, more than my mistakes.

A MOTHER'S PRAYER

Lord, help me to not take everything so personally. Give me the restraint to jump to justice when someone has wronged my daughter. Help me to be present in her hard and painful moments. Give me compassion and understanding. Lord, help me to have healthy boundaries for my heart and my time in a way she can understand. May I not replace You as her rock and the One she turns to when in need. In Jesus' name, Amen.

A Note from September

RAISING DAUGHTERS HAS CHANGED ME. I was broken and insecure, abandoned and afraid of making a whole mess of my daughters' lives. I made plenty of mistakes and continue to today. But here is one of the most important parts of my heart I want all mothers of daughters to know when they read my book: You are doing the best you can. Girls are complicated. We all are. If you want to do just one thing right, love them well. Let them know you will love them no matter what. Everything else will come together.

This book may be written as a "guide," but think of my words as a friend giving you the big picture. I would have given anything to have a mom by my side, as I fumbled my way through my motherhood journey. This was my turning point in mothering my daughters: knowing God has called me to so much more, and He calls me His beloved. This journey was painful and redemptive all at the same time.

This book isn't a list of dos and don'ts, with Bible verses thrown in. Every single word has been lived out in our day-to-day lives, and still is today. I often have to remind myself of the length of this journey and how far we've come. If I didn't have the Word of God and an identity rooted in Him, I would have been completely lost when my older daughters left home. I hope every mom who reads this will remember she is more than the daughters she has raised. Whatever the outcome, you are loved.

I am a mother just like you. There are days while raising girls that the noise and chatter wears on my nerves, and then there are days I hear them singing harmony in the bathroom together, while they are curling and braiding each other's hair, and I just smile with thankfulness. I experience hurt feelings from my daughters' words, and I hurt my daughters' hearts when I become busy, distracted, or tired of engaging in so many emotional conversations. I am navigating my way through new roles, busy lives, and trying to be present with everyone, for everyone. I love being a mom to girls, but it certainly takes a lot of work to wade through their opinions, choices, emotions, ideas, and reflections on how they were raised. My heart has learned to deflect guilt, and yet embrace the truth, even when it hurts. I've grown from mothering my girls out of fear and have found my peace and confidence in the choices I make.

As you close my book, I hope and pray you will find hope, beauty, and great excitement in your journey of raising girls. This is a lifelong journey you don't want to miss, so stay connected, keep turning to Jesus, and remember, He loves YOU no matter what!

September

Notes

1. Rosaria Butterfield, *The Gospel Comes with a House Key: Practicing Radically Ordinary Hospitality in Our Post-Christian World* (Crossway, 2018), 17.

2. Adapted from Lisa Tiano, "A Girl's Guide to Being a Good Friend," Her View from Home, https://herviewfromhome.com/a-girls-guide-to-being-a-good-friend/.

3. Sara Barratt, "Why Teens Have an Identity Crisis," The Gospel Coalition, July 12, 2022, https://www.thegospelcoalition.org/article/teens-identity-crisis/.

4. Kati Lynn Davis, "Preach the Gospel to Your Identity Crisis," Well-Watered Women, May 5, 2022, https://wellwateredwomen.com/preach-the-gospel-to-your-identity-crisis/.